WHAT YOUR COLLE.

Dr. Lionel E. Allen, Jr. is an educational leader who has always walked the walk. His knowledge comes from deep personal experience. He has dedicated his professional career to serving disadvantaged and marginalized students and communities. If you share his passion for that mission, I know you will find his insights both invaluable and inspiring.

—**Arne Duncan**, Former U.S. Secretary of Education, Washington, DC

Dr. Allen provides practical strategies for centering students' humanity, perspectives, and lived experiences to create culturally affirming educational spaces. This will require our educators to be courageous enough to show up differently. The strategies highlighted in this book are replicable and can be done tomorrow. This book also serves as a guide for parents, educational advocates, and community members on what they should be demanding from their schools.

—**Tiffany S. Brunson**, Superintendent, Elementary School District 159, Matteson, Illinois

Dr. Lionel Allen has provided mentoring and support for our area educational leaders for the past four years. During the darkest days of the pandemic, when our leaders were feeling defeated, Dr. Allen was a bright light that gave them hope and purpose. His passion and fearlessness in speaking the truth about our educational systems have inspired leaders to be innovators and intentional risk takers to ensure that every child experiences the Culture of C.A.R.E.

—**Jill Reedy**, Regional Superintendent of Schools, Decatur, Illinois

I have witnessed the administrative mastery of Dr. Lionel Allen in some of the most challenging schools and communities. He has produced excellence in places and spaces that many consider impossible to produce results. Dr. Allen provides a culturally responsive framework and clear, actionable strategies. This book is for educators and leaders who are serious about producing what Dr. Asa Hilliard called "excellence without excuses."

—**Chike Akua**, Assistant Professor of Educational Leadership, Clark Atlanta University, Author, *Education for Transformation: The Keys to Releasing the Genius of African American Students*, Atlanta, Georgia

Dr. Lionel Allen's book is an extraordinary tool for collective change. If teams of teachers and school leaders were to read and discuss Dr. Allen's book together, it is hard to imagine them emerging from the experience unmoved. It provides a mirror of school practices and mindsets that teachers and leaders will recognize, argue about, and from which they will inevitably learn.

—**Steven E. Tozer**, Professor Emeritus, University of Illinois Chicago, Oak Park, Illinois

This book is of tremendous value for educators and caretakers alike. With refreshing candor, Dr. Allen's no-nonsense approach makes a case that educators must care for their students. By confronting tired excuses for not caring, he reminds us of how simple caring can be, and the powerful impacts it has on students' lives.

—**Decoteau J. Irby**, Associate Professor, University of Illinois at Chicago, Chicago, Illinois

Lead With C.A.R.E.

To all those who felt school wasn't for them.

Lead With C.A.R.E.

Strategies to Build Culturally Competent and Affirming Schools

Lionel E. Allen, Jr.

Foreword by Gholdy Muhammad

For information:

Corwin
A Sage Company
2455 Teller Road
Thousand Oaks, California 91320
(800) 233-9936
www.corwin.com

Sage Publications Ltd.
1 Oliver's Yard
55 City Road
London EC1Y 1SP
United Kingdom

Sage Publications India Pvt. Ltd.
Unit No 323-333, Third Floor, F-Block
International Trade Tower Nehru Place
New Delhi 110 019
India

Sage Publications Asia-Pacific Pte. Ltd.
18 Cross Street #10-10/11/12
China Square Central
Singapore 048423

Printed in the United States of America

Paperback ISBN 978-1-0719-2501-0

This book is printed on acid-free paper.

Vice President and Editorial Director: Monica Eckman
Senior Acquisitions Editor: Tanya Ghans
Content Development Manager: Desirée A. Bartlett
Senior Editorial Assistant: Nyle De Leon
Production Editor: Vijayakumar
Copy Editor: Diane DiMura
Typesetter: TNQ Tech Pvt. Ltd.
Proofreader: Girish Sharma
Indexer: TNQ Tech Pvt. Ltd.
Cover Designer: Scott Van Atta
Marketing Manager: Melissa Duclos

24 25 26 27 28 10 9 8 7 6 5 4 3 2 1

Contents

CHAPTER FOUR

CHAPTER FIVE

CHAPTER SIX

Foreword

As a fifth grader whose family had just left Gary, Indiana for the suburbs of Illinois, I was nervous and scared to start a new school. In my new suburban school, I didn't see a teacher or student who looked like me or anyone who shared my cultural identities. When October came around, the teacher told each student that we had to dress up in costume for Halloween. I immediately felt tension and anxiety. I was a Muslim girl who didn't celebrate or dress up for Halloween. I felt pressure because the teacher told us we *had to* come in costume for the Halloween celebration as a requirement. In my determination to "fit in" and please the teacher, I used my saved money to purchase a costume from the local store. Not knowing how to select, I chose the size meant for a toddler. When I arrived at school, I was horrified when I didn't dress the part of the teacher's expectations and I certainly did not blend in with the other children. The embarrassment and lack of belonging were feelings that stayed with me throughout that school day—and I still remember them today.

This teacher must have seen my Muslim identity as a deficiency to overcome. She implicitly asked me to "check my Muslim" at the door because she only chose to honor and celebrate white, western holidays like Halloween and Christmas. Sadly, my teacher's practices were similar to practices in schools across the United States, where the curriculum, instruction, and leadership did not represent the diversity of the students, did not teach justice or anti-racism, did not offer linguistic or cultural inclusion, and did not teach anything but decontextualized skills. These same problems are still present in contemporary schools.

When I read Dr Allen's book on C.A.R.E., I can't help but think, *"What if my fifth-grade teacher had read this book and taught and led in culturally responsive ways—helping me, as a young Muslim girl, to understand, celebrate, know, and sustain my cultural identities? What if she had affirmed my identities and developed a beautiful loving relationship with me, creating spaces for me to empower myself?"* Dr. Allen provides a way to disrupt the harms that systems, teachers, and leaders may inflict on children. He uses the richness of his personal and professional experiences to speak to the true purpose and power of schools, which is to disrupt disparities and affirm students' cultural identities and brilliance. In doing so, Dr. Allen reminds educators that we must examine the structures of education historically and in the present so that we can dismantle harmful practices. Through the framework of C.A.R.E., he helps educators to lead with **C**ultural responsiveness in teaching and learning, while **A**ffirming children's identities and building positive **R**elationships with youth. He posits that this leads to spaces of **E**mpowerment. This book provides *the what, the why,* and, importantly, *the how.* The C.A.R.E. framework helps leaders center the genius and joy of youth and teachers, while recognizing the social times we live in and elevating the education of children, especially those who have been historically excluded in schooling and in society. The framework provides a way forward for leaders to lead differently—with care, belonging, and excellence; providing every child with what they deeply deserve.

Dr. Gholdy Muhammad
Associate Professor of Curriculum & Instruction
University of Illinois Chicago

Preface

On October 16, 1963, in the speech "The Negro Child—His Self Image," now known as "A Talk to Teachers," James Baldwin says, "The paradox of education is precisely this—that as one begins to become conscious, one begins to examine the society in which he is being educated." Baldwin argues that as we become more educated, we question and become critical of what we are and how we have been taught. I argue that the paradox of an educator is that the longer you work in education, the more you begin to examine, question, and refute the policies, practices, and structures that govern the educational system. I am a lifer. I have spent my entire professional existence in schools. I accepted my calling early and never wanted to do anything else. I am fortunate to get paid to do what I love, yet this work has been a tremendous source of disappointment and frustration.

This book is borne out of that frustration. As an educator for almost twenty-five years, I have grown increasingly tired of educational disproportionality, achievement disparities, and our stale attempts to address them. I am angered by the normalization of the failure of certain demographic groups of students and how quickly some educators absolve themselves of any responsibility. I am worried that despite improvements in teacher preparation, standards, and America's racial reckoning, deficit-minded orientations of historically marginalized children still prevail.

Yet, I am hopeful. This book is for the hopeful and courageous educator. This is for the leader and the teacher who understands that there is no panacea to the challenges we confront in education. They understand that improving schools for historically marginalized children will require the perfect mix of activism, urgency, and a willingness to reject desires for comfort. This book is not about strategy implementation; it is mostly about mindset shifts. Strategies are not enough. This book is for systems disruptors, individuals who understand that deep systemic change will not come from interventions, test prep programs, or new technologies but from educators willing to ask tough questions, interrogate the efficacy of traditional practices, and empower others to do the same.

There is nothing particularly earth-shattering in this book. Nothing hot, nothing super fresh, but it is very real. The strategies I suggest are simple; they require only commitment and intentionality. I do not pull punches or hide behind eduspeak; I write in ways that appeal to novice educators, veterans, parents, and students.

Critics will accuse me of blaming teachers, invalidating the successes achieved in education, and oversimplifying the challenges. They will say that there is nothing unique or different about what I offer. I say it is time to start pointing fingers, and our quest for something unique and fresh has confined us to a treadmill of ill-conceived reforms and poorly executed policies. Our lack of commitment and unwillingness to change are the root causes of the contaminated school cultures in which many students find themselves.

You will not agree with everything I write, and I am fine with that. I want you to feel angry, uncomfortable, and challenged. Lean fully into the discomfort and know that millions of students in schools nationwide feel uncomfortable. If your discomfort leads to a better experience for them, I have accomplished my mission.

Acknowledgments

The completion of this book would not have happened without the support of my wife and family. Fajr, every aspect of my life has improved because you are in it. Since we first met, you have always been one of my biggest champions. Thank you for believing in me when I did not always believe in myself. I want to thank my boys for the honor of being your Pop. Your futures burn bright with promise, and I cannot wait to see what will come. My heart bursts with joy and pride because of you all. Ma, thank you for being the living embodiment of love and commitment. I shudder at the thought of where Brandon and I would be without you. I am still only now learning the extent of your sacrifices. Where you sent me to school changed my life. I love you. Dad, I miss you and love you. Thank you for breaking the cycle. To my brother, Brandon, words cannot capture my love and appreciation for you. Our bond is unbreakable.

I want to thank Dr. Decoteau Irby for his friendship, mentorship, and support. I am not sure this book would have happened without your unwavering encouragement and push. Thanks also to my colleagues at the University of Illinois at Chicago, particularly the good people in the College of Education and the Urban Education Leadership EdD program. My experiences as a graduate student and now a faculty member have greatly shaped me, and I am grateful for the blessing that UIC has been to me.

To the team at Corwin, thanks so much for helping to bring this book to life. I am grateful to Tanya Ghans for responding to my initial email and for taking the time to listen to my (not fully baked) vision for this project, for your support, and straightforward feedback. This book only happens with your advocacy. Desirée A. Bartlett and Nyle De Leon, thank you for your patience as you guided me through the production process. Your kind spirit and accessibility made this journey less stressful than I anticipated. Diane DiMura, thanks for the gift of your eagle eye. I do not know how you do what you do, but I am thankful to have you as a part of the team. Thanks also to the marketing team for your support with this project.

Finally, I must thank ALL the excellent educators with whom I have had the opportunity to share the schoolhouse, teach, coach, and support. Throughout my career, I have benefitted greatly from being in the presence of great teachers and leaders. I have learned a great deal from being in community with you. This book is for you!

PUBLISHER'S ACKNOWLEDGMENTS

Corwin gratefully acknowledges the contributions of the following reviewers:

Peter Dillon, Superintendent
Berkshire Hills Regional District
Stockbridge, Massachusetts

Louis Lim, Principal
York Region District School Board
Ontario, Canada

Joy Rose, Retired High School Principal,
Worthington, Ohio

Catherine Sosnowski, Adjunct Professor
Central Connecticut State University
New Britain, Connecticut

About the Author

A native of the southside of Chicago, **Dr. Lionel E. Allen, Jr.** is a clinical assistant professor of educational policy studies at the University of Illinois at Chicago (UIC), where he teaches a signature pedagogy course on cycles of inquiry, organizational change, and coleads the full-year residency course for aspiring school leaders. Lionel has over twenty years of experience as a teacher, assistant principal, principal, and chief academic officer. He is an education reform consultant, principal coach, and a frequently invited speaker. In 2005, former CPS CEO and United States Secretary of Education Arne Duncan selected Lionel to become the first turnaround principal in Illinois. Under his leadership, the Sherman School of Excellence went from the second-worst performing school in the state to become a national model and a catalyst for future school reform efforts. He recently detailed this experience in the book *Fighting the Good Fight: Narratives of the African American Principalship* (2022) in a chapter titled "How Should I Feel About That? Renaissance 2010 and School Reform in Chicago." Lionel is the founder of ed Leaders Matter (eLM), LLC, a consultancy that aims to improve schools by developing school leaders. Under the eLM umbrella, Lionel has provided professional development and coaching to hundreds of school leaders and scores of schools and school districts nationwide. He is also the cofounder and design team member of the Aspire Fellowship, a program designed to diversify the principal pipeline by preparing teacher leaders of color to enter into principal preparation and certification programs. Lionel received his baccalaureate degree from Northwestern University and his master's and doctoral degrees from University of Illinois at Chicago. Lionel Allen works with educators! Learn more at www.letsleadwithCARE.com

Introduction to the Framework: Making the Case for a Culture of C.A.R.E.

LEARNING GOALS

As a result of reading this chapter, educators will:

☐ Understand the power of school culture to transform lives.

☐ Know the four pillars of the Culture of C.A.R.E. Framework.

☐ Understand the Culture of C.A.R.E. Framework's theory of action.

SCHOOL SAVED ME

I grew up on the southeast side of Chicago in the late 1980s and early 1990s. If you know anything about Chicago at that time, you know that the crack epidemic, gang violence, and disinvestment plagued most African American and Latinx communities and the schools within them. I was in third grade in 1987 when then U.S. Secretary of Education William Bennett made headlines by labeling Chicago Public Schools as the worst school district in the nation (Banas & Byers, 1987). Knowing that I grew up during this time and under these conditions, you might assume that I attended underfunded, underresourced schools with dejected teachers who did not care about me. You might speculate that I sat in classes where it was nearly impossible to learn and that I graduated college and earned advanced degrees *despite* my educational experiences. If you thought this was my story, you would not be alone, but you would be wrong.

School saved me. Yes, I was born to a mother who did not attend college and a father who was pushed out of high school by his sophomore year (more on that later), and yes, I was reared in a neighborhood plagued by violence and drugs, and yes, some of my closest friends were gang members. Like many African American males who grow up in neighborhoods like mine, by the age of 21, I could name more than a few friends and acquaintances who were dead or in jail, and yes, I, too, was tempted by the allure of the fast life on the streets. Maybe if I could just sell dope for a few weeks, or months I could alleviate some of my mom's financial burdens, and maybe I would no longer have to hear her cry from the stress of not being able to pay the bills, but school saved me.

My life today differs greatly from many of the young men and women I grew up with. I am no more talented, intelligent, or gifted than they are. In fact, one could argue that despite our struggles, they did more with less, were more resilient, and certainly were more street savvy than I ever was. We hung out on the same corners, sat on the same porches, played ball on the same courts and fields, ran through the same alleys, and bought snacks and junk food from the same corner stores, but there was one glaring difference—the schools we attended. I never attended my neighborhood schools. As I reflect on my life and the lives of my peers, one could surmise that "success" in life was contingent on the quality of the schools you attended. In Chicago at that time, families had three educational options: They could send their child to the school in their attendance boundary (neighborhood school), they could have their child tested for admittance into a magnet or gifted program, or they could pay to send their child to a private school. For a myriad of reasons, the quality of traditional public education began to wane in the 1980s and 1990s. Thankfully, I was born to parents who were savvy enough to explore the educational options available to me and committed to navigating the labyrinth of Chicago Public Schools, guiding me down a path that would alter the trajectory of my life forever.

Even as a child, I knew that my elementary school experiences were different from most of my friends. When we talked about school, they often complained about how dirty their buildings were and how their teachers did not care about them. They could not bring their books home because there were not enough for every student to have one, so they did not have to carry bookbags. They rarely took field trips because their teachers thought they were "too bad," and it appeared that fights and other serious disruptions to the learning environment were a common occurrence. Meanwhile, I had a tremendously rich school experience. In elementary school, my teachers had high expectations of me and my classmates. I did not like all my teachers, but I never questioned if they cared about me or wanted me to do well. I had teachers who I thought were mean because they had surly dispositions, assigned too much homework, or made us stand up in class when we were caught talking. Our school was clean, our books were old, but everyone had their own, so we were able to take them home to complete our homework. Even though I blossomed to six feet by seventh grade, I was never treated as if athletics were my only option. Thomas Little, the assistant principal at my elementary school, was an African American male. He took a personal interest in not just me but other young men in my school (African American and Latino) who, from time to time, needed tough love, redirection, and a restatement of expectations. Mr. Little continues to be one of my biggest supporters and a major reason why I went into education.

In high school, the teachers who cared pushed me intellectually and refused to accept anything less than my best. They made me feel smart and encouraged me to take Honors and AP courses. There was urgency in their approach to preparing me for college and for life beyond school. We were empowered to pursue our academic and extracurricular interests. Excellence was the standard, and the question was not if, but where, you were going to go to college. There were multiple opportunities for us to feel connected to the school. This, unfortunately, was very different from the experiences of many of my friends from the neighborhood. School saved me.

I am writing this book because if school could save me, then it can save others. Education is often championed as the great equalizer, and we know the historical significance educational institutions have had in marginalized communities of color. Unfortunately, educational institutions have not always lived up to this standard. Many students, particularly African American and Latinx students, and their families, do not view schools as places that empower them and affirm their brilliance; they view them as demoralizing institutions that are hell-bent on maintaining compliance and order and not on maximizing student potential.

THE CASE FOR A CULTURE OF C.A.R.E.

It is sobering and unfortunate that anyone has to argue about the importance of making our students feel loved, cared for, and valued in schools. That should be a given. For many students, however, it is not. Students across our nation—African American, Latinx, poor, pick a label—do not feel cared for in schools. They do not see the relevance of the school experience—what they are asked to learn, read, do—to their daily lives. They do not see themselves represented in the curriculum; they are not allowed to explore their interests; and they struggle connecting with the adults who are charged with their social, emotional, and academic development. It is this reality that leads to high rates of disengagement, disciplinary issues, and subpar rates of achievement. Like adults who do not feel valued, or appreciated at work, students struggle when they are not happy in school. Despite what some educational hard-liners think, school should be a place where students find joy (Muhammad, 2020), where they are allowed to make mistakes, test boundaries, and have fun—at all grade levels. Unfortunately, as I visit schools across the country where the majority of students are African American and Latinx, I see the absence of joy and the intentional removal of fun. I see an overemphasis on *safety,* a term that serves as a proxy and justification for overly punitive disciplinary policies and the overpolicing of Black and Brown bodies.

The key to improving student experiences directly and student performance indirectly is to adopt a mindset that centers the care of and the care for our students over everything else.

> We can, whenever and wherever we choose, successfully teach all children whose schooling is of interest to us. We already know more than we need to do that. Whether or not we do it must finally depend on how we feel about the fact that we haven't so far.
>
> **—Dr. Ron Edmonds, 1979**

As Dr. Ron Edmonds says, educators know what to do to educate our students properly, but have yet to exhibit the kind of courage and will to act upon these core beliefs. Transforming schools requires a wholesale change to our approach and collective mindsets. The COVID-19 pandemic and the United States' racial reckoning gave hope to many that the educational community would begin to critically examine its systems, policies, and practices to improve the academic experiences of students of color, particularly African American students. We heard a call to "reimagine education." Remote learning brought educators into students' homes, and with that came a deluge of empathy, understanding, and care at previously unseen levels. Schools and school districts responded to student and family needs quickly and with a level of urgency commiserate with the crisis at hand. Tragically, as we returned to normal, we have not heeded Winston Churchill's call to "never let a good crisis go to waste" and—despite the call to "reinvent education"—have reverted to our old ways, despite their ineffectiveness. The hope that the pandemic would catalyze educational innovation has died due to the system's fixation on comfort and habit. Out of one side of our mouths, we champion education reform; out of the other, there is an outright refusal to interrogate the cultural norms, attitudes, mindsets, and habits that govern students' experiences. What is not often acknowledged is that many marginalized students excelled during remote learning in large part due to a focus on socioemotional learning, the absence of racialized micro-aggressions, and the implementation of policies and practices that minimized the emphasis on grading. The laser-like focus on quantifiable results has returned and continues to drastically undermine the experiences of all students, particularly marginalized student groups. Results are important, but the prioritization of student outcomes over student experiences has created stifling, suffocating school experiences whereby many students of color feel either overpoliced or invisible.

NO CHILD LEFT BEHIND

No Child Left Behind (NCLB) was the catalyst of the "results over everything" culture. The charge to ensure that by the year 2014, every child would be able to read and do math at grade level was a noble one. What was not considered was how school districts would respond to the call. This pressure for arbitrary proficiency created a culture of accountability (bad accountability, not good accountability) and fear, and took the fun out of school. Schools responded to NCLB by creating developmentally inappropriate learning environments for students. No schools felt the pressure and suffered more from NCLB than schools serving poor communities of color. The threat of probation, closure, and state takeover thrust districts into a reactionary, survival mode, leading to poor decision-making and ill-fated policies. Policies that fundamentally altered the experience that children had in schools were implemented in places like New York, Los Angeles, Baltimore, and Chicago. Many teachers lost the ability to bring joy and creativity to their lessons. Students became data points on a spreadsheet. The school became synonymous with test prep. Students who did not test well were placed in intervention or special education classes. Principals and teachers were pressured to improve test scores and were celebrated for test performance boosts despite some who employed practices that were detrimental to students. Elective classes were often eliminated to provide additional time to focus on reading, writing, and mathematics. The key to success, many school leaders thought, was to drill and kill students in basic skills. In Chicago, generations of students never had science, social studies, or art classes because the day was divided into halves. Reading often took place in the morning and math in the afternoon (these were the two subjects that determined NCLB status). Schools became overly punitive because "bad" students negatively affected test scores. Disruptive students were excluded instead of supported. Suspensions and expulsions increased, and marginalized students suffered the most. Results were all that mattered regardless of the cost.

What many educators and educational policymakers have refused to accept is, despite conventional wisdom, teachers and leaders do not control results. Despite the value we attach to them, standardized tests are produced by for-profit companies and paint, at best, an incomplete picture and, at worst, an inaccurate picture of what a student knows and can do. Oppressive rituals like standardized testing and tracking coupled with punitive and exclusionary disciplinary practices destroy what should be rich and rewarding academic experiences for students. The results-driven and high achievement-at-all-cost cultures that plague many schools and school districts fuel educational inequities and jeopardize students' social, emotional, and intellectual health. African American, Latinx, and other marginalized student groups like diverse learners, English Language learners (ELLs), and students who live in poverty find themselves victims of school practices and school cultures that fail to meet their needs adequately.

The framework I am advancing in this book is the potential cure for this sickness. Schools that enact this framework have established and sustained a culture that rests upon four essential pillars: cultural responsiveness, affirmation, relationship-building, and empowerment.

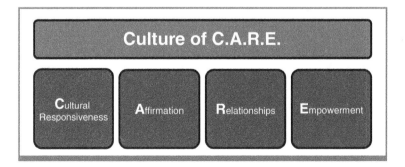

I, and many other students from historically marginalized communities have directly benefited from schools and school communities who prioritize these pillars as foundational to the student experience. The words they use may be different, but the meaning and the impact of these pillars are similar.

> If a farmer is tryin' to grow corn and the corn don't grow, he don't blame the corn.
>
> —Sharecropper

This book is not about boosting test scores or other quantifiable metrics. I will not encourage you to set goals to improve your school's performance in these areas. Test scores, attendance rates, and so on are lagging indicators, they give us an assessment of how our schools are performing right now based on the current state of practices, operations, and resources. I challenge you to focus on the leading indicators: the mindsets we must have, the habits and behaviors we must employ, and the systems we need to disrupt. This is important because it is not the backgrounds of the students or the lack of resources and technology that are the causes of the most predominant issues in education. It is our collective mindsets and the systems that we maintain that are the root causes of the problems. As James Clear (2018) says in *Atomic Habits*, "If you want better results, then forget about setting goals. Focus on your systems instead. Goals are good for setting a direction, but systems are for making progress." Disrupt the systems and change our mindsets and then and only then will we accomplish what we say we want to accomplish.

As a wise sharecropper once stated, "If a farmer is tryin' to grow corn and the corn don't grow, he don't blame the corn." Educational leaders and teachers must adopt that same mindset. Many of our students are struggling to grow academically, socially, and emotionally because the soil of our schools (the culture) is toxic. Nothing grows in a toxic environment. Improving our schools requires that we improve the experiences that our students are having; improving those experiences requires educators to drastically improve the culture of the school. This is what we do have control over not test results, but the experiences we offer children and the culture we create. Culture is the soil in which everything in a school grows from. Show me a sick, dysfunctional school plagued by achievement disparities, disengagement, and discontent and I will show you an unhealthy school culture.

THE C.A.R.E. FRAMEWORK THEORY OF ACTION

IF schools establish a culture built on **C**ultural responsiveness, **A**ffirmation, **R**elationships, and **E**mpowerment, THEN they will dramatically improve the academic experiences of often marginalized student groups, leading to improved outcomes.

I wrote this introduction to the book (Chapter 1) just shy of the two-year anniversary of the death of my dad. One of the smartest men that I knew, he discontinued his traditional and formal education after his sophomore year of high school. When asked why he stopped attending school he said, "School wasn't for cats like me." As I write this book, I think about his contemporaries, brilliant men, and women with many talents who also felt unwelcome and unwanted in schools. I think about the generations of youngsters that would come after him feeling the same way he did about school. Young people who longed for but never felt seen in school. They never saw themselves represented in the curriculum, never felt affirmed by their teachers, did not have authentic caring relationships with the adults responsible for their development, and often felt disempowered in schools. I think about the young men and women who, despite their intelligence, resilience, and talents, have opted not to attend school, not because they did not value education but because the institution that was responsible for their education did not value them. Young men and women who did not drop out but were pushed out.

A FEW WORDS OF CAUTION

Yes, I Am Angry

If, as you read this book, you feel that I am angry, frustrated, and disappointed, then you would be right. At some point, educators must decide whether we are willing to do what it takes to do right for *all* children. We have an industry overloaded with consultants, experts, and the newest and hottest technology, but we still cannot seem to find ways to provide every child, regardless of skin color, zip code, or level of poverty, a high-quality, empowering, and liberating educational experience. How can we not all be angry?

I Love School Leaders and Teachers, But Not All of Them

I do not want anyone to feel as if I am bashing all educators in this book, but I am bashing some. Teaching is a noble profession, and I am grateful to teachers and leaders who have chosen to stay in the field despite the difficulties plaguing us. The polarization, the political divisiveness, and the attacks on historical truths have made professions associated with education less desirable than they have ever been. I am both thankful and grateful for those who do this work for the right reasons and center on what is best for children over the convenience and comfort of adults. Once while leading a professional development session, a department chair admitted in a public forum that he allows some of his teachers to harm students. His justification for this educational malpractice was that he only has to work with the student for a year or two but he must see the teacher every day for twenty to twenty-five years. His comfort and his friendships with his colleagues were more important than the well-being of his students. I do not love that educator.

I Am Not Concerned With Anyone's Readiness

You will not agree with everything that is written in this book and I am fine with that. We are the sum of our lived experiences and as Anais Nin (2014) stated, "We do not see the world as it is, we see it as we are." My experiences as a teacher, school leader, network leader, and now professor and consultant have shaped my perspective in very particular ways. In my attempt to make the case for the importance of establishing a Culture of C.A.R.E., I illuminate some problematic mindsets, behaviors, and practices. This could be perceived as me beating up on school leaders and teachers. That is not my intention. My intention is to hold all of us accountable to doing better by children. This requires us to engage in critical self-reflection and be honest and courageous enough with ourselves to reflect on (a) how we are contributing to the problem, and (b) what we need to do differently. As a turn-around principal in Chicago, I employed practices that I am embarrassed about. I did things and acted in ways that are counter to the type of educator I aspired to be. It is uncomfortable for me to admit, but step 1 to becoming a better leader or teacher is to confront what is most ugly about our thoughts and behaviors and commit to changing ourselves. Before we can change and trans-form schools we must change and transform ourselves. Only you know if you are ready for that, but I am not concerned about your or anyone else's readiness when generations of children are being harmed because we lack collective courage and have decided that our readiness trumps what is best for children.

STRUCTURE

This book is divided into six chapters. A brief synopsis of each is as follows:

Chapter 1: Introduction: Making the Case for a Culture of C.A.R.E.

In this first chapter, I have attempted to make the case for establishing a Culture of C.A.R.E. Each subsequent chapter will be devoted to a pillar of the framework beginning with cultural responsiveness.

Chapter 2: Cultural Responsiveness

To be culturally responsive is to create a school and classroom environment that acknowledges, responds to, and celebrates the diversity of students' cultures in meaningful ways and offers full, equitable access to education for all students. School leaders, faculty, and staff recognize the importance of including students' cultural references in all aspects of learning (Ladson-Billings, 1994). This chapter will explain what it means to establish a culturally responsive school and classroom. Drawing on the early work of scholars like Dr. Gloria Ladson-Billings and Dr. Geneva Gay, readers will be challenged to rethink how to operationalize cultural responsiveness in their schools and classrooms.

Chapter 3: Affirmation

To affirm a student is to celebrate, honor, protect, and cultivate their identity. To affirm a student is to nurture, love, and value their uniqueness and validate their sense of self; to offer emotional support or encouragement. This chapter presents practical, research-informed strategies to ensure school leaders and teachers are affirming the identities and acknowledging the humanity in every child they encounter. The pressures of social media, the stresses associated with the pandemic, and an ever-decisive world, require that educators are intentional about elevating the self-esteem and self-worth of the students they serve. Many students particularly, African American, and Latinx students are made to feel inferior, effectively souring their academic experiences and pushing them away from schools.

Chapter 4: Relationships

If this was a book about real estate investing, I would be championing the phrase "Location, location, location"; because this is a book about school culture and supporting student success, I must champion the phrase "Relationships, relationships, relationships." Calling educators to invest in building relationships with their students is not new but what is often missing from that conversation is the work that leaders and teachers must engage in to build the relationship. In this chapter, I not only make the case for relationship building but how to do it. I will challenge readers to rethink how they interact with and forge bonds with students, to reflect on ways they may have undermined relationships, and to offer concrete relationship-building strategies that can be leveraged immediately in their schools.

Chapter 5: Empowerment

Many students view schools as disempowering and joyless places. Too many schools have become places where random and arbitrary knowledge is deposited into the minds of students, and only compliant students who can regurgitate often useless information are seen as successful. School, for many students, is a place where they first learn what they cannot be and where they first learn that they are not good enough. To address this heartbreaking reality, schools must be intentional about empowering students. When schools are committed to empowering students, they help them realize their abilities and potential and grant them the power and authority to be great. In this chapter, I will offer concrete strategies to help educators empower their students to realize their full potential.

Chapter 6: Conclusion

The conclusion will remind readers of the importance of school culture in defining the in-school experiences of students. It will challenge them to reject the idea that educators must only be driven by results and to acknowledge that when it comes to educating children, we only have control over what happens within the four walls of our schools and our classrooms. Rejecting the "achievement at all costs" mindset frees educators to do what is best in classrooms which is to create warm, caring, loving spaces where students feel loved, cared for, emotionally and physically safe, and intellectually challenged. Results will come, but we must first focus on what is important: school culture.

Each chapter will end with a summary and five reflection questions.

WHY THIS BOOK NOW?

I am writing this book because it is time for educators to realize the responsibility that they have for why things are the way that they are. This book is not about assigning blame or rehashing the problem without providing solutions. Those of us who have spent more than ten minutes in education know how skilled we are in articulating problems but how shallow our solutions are. Rather than look inward for the solutions to achievement disparities, lack of student engagement, poor attendance, and disproportionalities that exist in our schools, we (a) do nothing about it because this is how things have always been or (b) latch on to the new hot thing. Neither approach has led to sustainable improvement. The Culture of C.A.R.E. Framework is different in that it rests almost solely on the need for educators to shift their mindsets. It requires school leaders and teachers to think differently about their role in improving the lives of their most marginalized students. It places the responsibility for school improvement at the feet of the educator, not parents, not political officials, not researchers, nor consultants. I believe wholeheartedly in the power of the principal and the teacher to transform the lives of students. I know how powerfully positive academic experiences can significantly alter the trajectory of a child's life, and I have also witnessed how negative or traumatic school experiences can harm a student, robbing them of the self-sufficiency, confidence, and esteem that they need to navigate the complexities of our world. I have seen how schools can ruin a child's life, push them away, and condemn them to a life of struggle. Typically, when authors pen books like this, they do so to document an overwhelmingly negative experience that they had to overcome. Through grit, resilience, and good fortune, they were able to overcome insurmountable obstacles to reach success and they write and often speak about those horrible experiences as a warning to educators about what not to do. They are also written to inspire educators to take greater care and responsibility for those students. Leveraging these experiences, they then reverse engineer what can and should be done in schools for young people. This book is different. I do not have a sob story to share about my school experience. I had a wonderful academic experience (which as an African American male, some might find hard to believe). In fact, school for me was an escape from a sometimes stressful childhood. The school was an extension of my home—a place where I felt loved and cared for. It was a place that made me feel good about being me. It was a place where I was challenged intellectually and held accountable for my learning and my behaviors. It was a place where nothing less than my best was accepted. I was able to thrive in my school and that is precisely why I am writing this book.

As I mentioned before, we spend so much time detailing all that is wrong in the field of education, and we do not spend nearly as much time detailing all that is right. Is our educational system broken? No, it is not—more on that later. Are African American, Latinx, female students, and other marginalized groups receiving the same caliber of education as their white peers? Nope. Are there some schools that are educating marginalized groups well? Yep. Have you ever heard about them? Probably not.

The best thing—and most challenging thing—about this book is that it reminds educators that the solutions for much of what plague our schools are free and lie within educators themselves. Success does not require the retention of expensive consultants, new technology, or hours of boring professional development. It does, however, require us to acknowledge the importance of school culture in our work and that our ways of thinking, believing, existing, and engaging with one another and our students are either promoting or inhibiting the success of our students. This book is about school culture—not curriculum, instruction, formative assessments, or summative assessments. This book is about how we, as an educational collective, can work to transform school cultures in a way that will lead to the success of all students (even our most marginalized). If we have learned anything, we should have learned that school improvement strategies alone have not been able to guarantee sustainable school improvement.

I encourage you to fully engage with this book. Mark it up, argue with it, challenge the thinking, but above all, reflect on your practice.

CHAPTER 1 SUMMARY

- When adults intentionally build a positive school culture that prioritizes the needs of students, schools can transform lives.

- Improving students' academic performance requires educators to improve their academic experiences.

- Improving students' academic experiences requires that educators adopt a mindset that prioritizes the care of and the care for the students they serve.

- School leaders must be willing to resist the "results over everything" culture that has permeated the educational landscape.

- A Culture of C.A.R.E. rests on the four pillars of cultural responsiveness, affirmation, relationships, and empowerment.

REFLECTION QUESTIONS

1. Beyond academics, what role did the schoolhouse play in your life? Did you succeed because of or despite of the schools you attended?

2. Do you agree with the theory of action advanced in this chapter? Why or why not?

3. What are the barriers to addressing the needs of the whole child?

4. At first glance, which pillars of the Culture of C.A.R.E. framework resonate with you most? Why?

5. Are you ready to reflect on and deeply examine your mindset and assumptions regarding educating historically marginalized students?

The "C": Cultural Responsiveness

LEARNING GOALS

As a result of reading this chapter, educators will:

☐ Understand the meaning of cultural responsiveness.

☐ Know how the "Ugly Truths" serve as barriers to meeting the needs of all students.

☐ Be able to implement culturally responsive practices in their schools.

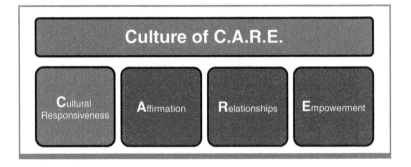

Cultural responsiveness is one of those ubiquitous and ambiguous terms in education, like *rigor*, *differentiation*, and *equity*, which are often used but rarely understood. The terms *culturally responsive* and *culturally relevant* emerged from the research of scholars Geneva Gay and Gloria Ladson Billings who sought to codify the practices and approaches of successful teachers of students of color-African American students in particular. Ladson-Billings helped us to understand that while best-in-class strategies were essential, it was the heart of these teachers that drove their practice. They loved and cared for their students. They were not just names on the roster or vessels to deposit knowledge. These teachers saw their students as brilliant and talented and worthy of support, and nurturing. They saw themselves in their students and believed it was their responsibility to positively shape the lives of their students. Regardless of their home lives and the unique circumstances their students often found themselves in, these teachers maintained high expectations of their students and believed they had assets they could leverage in meaningful ways to enrich their academic experiences and those of their peers.

Ladson-Billings (1994) says to be culturally responsive is to create a school and classroom environment that acknowledges, responds to, and celebrates the diversity of students' cultures in meaningful ways and offers full, equitable access to education for all students. Culturally responsive school leaders, teachers, and staff recognize the importance of including students' cultural references in all aspects of learning. Despite claims that schools are not designed to be culturally responsive and that educators need more training on becoming more culturally responsive, the reality is that schools and the adults who work in them are indeed culturally responsive.

Schools are designed to respond to the culture of white, Christian, middle-class families. Everything from how school calendars are constructed, to celebrated holidays, to curriculum materials, to norms for student behavior are based on white, Christian, middle-class values. Without launching into a discussion of the history of public education in the United States, we know that the function of schools and how they operate has not changed since their inception in the 1800s (Labaree, 2010; Rose, 2012); we also know that when those schools were designed, they did not take into consideration the needs of African Americans, Latinx, working moms, or nontraditional families. The systems and structures we inherited in our schools from previous generations of educators were not designed to address the needs of the diverse students in our schools. Despite demographic shifts, we have failed to shift our practices. As of the Fall of 2021, more than 50% of students in U.S. public schools are African American, Latinx, Asian, mixed race, or Native American (National Center for Education Statistics [NCE], 2023). The world has changed, yet the way we do the business of schooling has not.

THE UGLY TRUTHS

When making a case for why cultural responsiveness is necessary, I will begin with what I call the "ugly truths." These truths help us understand why we have not made the requisite shifts but also (hopefully) raise our collective sense of urgency around why cultural responsiveness is necessary. Owning these truths is the first step toward becoming a more culturally responsive educator.

Ugly Truth #1: There Are Systems in Place That Create and Reinforce Inequities That Lead to the Oppression of Historically Marginalized (Particularly African American and Latinx) People

Culturally responsive educators have to be willing to acknowledge that most, if not all, U.S. systems were designed to reinforce inequities and oppress people of color, African Americans in particular (Ewing, 2018; Irby, 2021; Khalifa, 2018). African

American people pay more in taxes, more for insurance, attend worse schools, and have constrained access to quality health care (Bonilla-Silva, 2010; Wilkerson, 2020). This is a fact, not an opinion. That's not to say that the tax attorneys, the insurance agents, the teachers, and the doctors who work in these systems are racist. As Bonilla-Silva (2014) asserts, racism persists in U.S. society even though most Americans self-identify as non-racist. Racism, as Eve Ewing (2018) reminds us in her book *Ghosts in the Schoolyard*, does not just live within individuals; it lives in the systems; it lives in the very fabric of U.S. society. This is why our society "consistently follows a pattern, churning out different outcomes for different people in ways that are linked to race" (p. 12).

Ugly Truth #2: We Have All Been Socialized Into Believing in the Inherent Inferiority of People of Color (Non-whites), Particularly African American People

A culturally responsive educator acknowledges Ugly Truth #2. All Americans are taught that African American and Latinx people are less human than others. This narrative that African American people are inherently inferior was necessary to justify their oppression, subjugation, and enslavement. This persists today as schools, mass media, and social media continue to advance this notion that African American people are less intelligent, less hardworking, more susceptible to deviance and criminality, and less trustworthy. We are all socialized this way. This is why white educators often fear their African American students. It is also why teachers struggle to see the inherent brilliance in their students of color and the assets in the communities they serve. African American educators struggle with this as well. After graduating from college and earning graduate degrees, they often find themselves adopting the same values as their white coworkers and adopting the same types of "pull yourself up by your bootstraps," or "I made it, so can you," mindsets that are inherently problematic. African American educators will often begin to develop an identity where they see themselves as better than the families and the communities they serve. This leads to the last of the ugly truths.

Ugly Truth #3: School Cultures Are Hostile Toward Minoritized Students

Achievement and discipline data support the fact that school cultures are hostile toward minoritized students (Khalifa, 2018). African American and Latinx students often experience schools as disempowering, disconnected, joyless places. They are often constrained from accessing the full depth and breadth of the academic curriculum, are disconnected from the rich social aspects of schooling, are overly disciplined, and are suspended and expelled from schools at six to seven times the rate of their white peers. That, coupled with the fact that there is such a dearth of African American and Latinx educators in schools, they struggled to find people who look like them to forge a personal connection with. Culturally responsive educators must acknowledge the history of oppression and marginalization that has taken place in our schools, a history that has drastically undermined the experiences of African American and Latinx students.

PURPOSE

The purpose of this chapter is to share concrete practices that educators can begin to implement tomorrow without having to register for another professional development course or invest thousands of dollars on curriculum materials and new technology. What is most required of educators is a shift in mindset. This mindset shift forces educators to engage in what Muhammad Khalifa (2018) calls "critical self-reflection." More broadly, it requires educators to reject the othering of students and families and be willing to problematize our systems and deeply interrogate what we do in our schools and why we do it. Historically in education, we engage in behavior and practices simply because "we have always done it that way." When our results are not what we want them to be, rather than ask ourselves, *What could we have done differently?* we blame the unintended outcomes on our students (kid blaming) and their families. We consistently, year after year, decade after decade, do what we have always done and expect that, somehow the results will be different. We do not thoroughly examine the effectiveness of our practices because doing so might reveal a need to change them. Changing our practices would force us out of our comfort zones and schools are nothing if not bastions of adult comfort. Comfort has always been the enemy to progress. A reason why schools have failed to respond to the needs of students en masse is because of the desire of many educators, teachers and principals alike to hold on to past practices and strategies that are outdated and ineffective.

EXAMINING MISCONCEPTIONS

Before launching into a discussion of how to operationalize cultural responsiveness, let us address a few misconceptions.

Misconception #1: "I Don't Know How to Be Culturally Responsive"

Yes, you do. Every educator is a culturally responsive educator. The question is, as Ladson-Billings asks, whose culture are you responding to? Many educators are unwilling to and uncomfortable with responding to the needs of students for which they feel no cultural connection to or responsibility for. It is easier to feign ignorance, than to admit, I am uncomfortable teaching these students.

Misconception #2: "I Need a List of Strategies to Become a Culturally Responsive Educator"

No, you do not. Being a culturally responsive educator is not about strategies and behaviors. It is about what is in your heart and mind. Leaders and teachers who have a track record of success with African American, Latinx students, and other marginalized students do not point to a particular book, class, or Ted Talk for their awakening. They point to their passion, commitment, and dedication to all students. As a teacher, I had very little in common with my white students who lived in mansions and summered in the Hamptons. I did not, however, allow our dissimilar cultural experiences to justify disconnecting from them as their teacher. It just meant I had to work harder to forge relationships with my students.

Misconception #3: "All of This Talk About Cultural Responsiveness Focuses Too Much on African American and Latinx Students"

And we should be! They are being failed by school systems that have subjugated and oppressed them. However, culturally responsive mindset shifts, and practical strategies are applicable to all marginalized groups. Find the most marginalized groups in your school and leverage some of these practices; you will be amazed at the impact they will have.

Misconception #4: "With All That I Have on My Plate, I Do Not Have Time to Learn the Culture of All the Students I Teach"

Find another job. If an African American teacher said that they could not effectively teach white students because they do not have time to learn white culture they would be dismissed immediately. Such a statement would be deemed educational treason, yet non-African American and Latinx leaders and teachers reflect this sentiment in both words and actions. Being a culturally responsive educator is so much more than knowing the latest hip hop songs, making TikTok videos, or understanding the latest slang. It takes commitment and dedication to your craft and a willingness to connect with students and their families.

CONCRETE PRACTICES FOR OPERATIONALIZING CULTURAL RESPONSIVENESS

The aim of this section is to demonstrate what culturally responsiveness looks like in a school. Here, I seek to provide concrete practices that educators can employ to become more culturally responsive. This list is not exhaustive. It is my attempt to bridge the gap between the theoretical, that is, our intellectual understanding of the concept, and the practical, what it looks like in practice.

Culturally Responsive Practice #1: Shadow a Student

In education, we spend and unfortunately waste a lot of money on professional development. The field is rife with consultants, experts, trainers, and developers, many of whom have spent little if any time actually working in schools. Year after year, decade after decade we invest heaps of money on "professional learning," attending conferences, participating in book talks, and more, yet this investment yields few, if any, substantive practice changes. I will save my diatribe about poor quality professional development and share a strategy that aspiring culturally responsive educators can employ tomorrow, for free: shadowing a student.

As a leader, shadowing a student was one of the most powerful professional learning experiences I have ever had. Before discussing its potency, let me define what I mean by shadowing a student. First, you must clear your schedule for the day. If you are principal or assistant principal, you want your team to behave as if you are out of the office (you are not available that day); if you are a teacher or staff member, you need to make sure your classes and other duties are covered for the day. Second, you must select a student. You can randomly choose a student, or if you are interested in observing the experiences of a particular type of student (i.e., African American, Latinx, Advanced Placement, English Language Learner, or diverse learners), select a student that will allow you to sufficiently observe those experiences. After clearing your day and selecting your student, follow that student the entire day, beginning with their first period class all the way through dismissal. Whether you choose to eat lunch in the student cafeteria is up to you. Trust me when I say that you will learn so much from this experience. Seeing the school from the students' perspective is a powerful experience. The learning is rich and educative. I shadowed a student when I served as chief academic officer (CAO) of a network of charter high schools and here is just a snippet of what I learned:

- The day is excessively long; I was exhausted at the end of the school day.
- Overall, my students were well behaved.
- Out of seven academic classes, I noticed quality instruction in only two of them.
- Most of the classes I attended were boring.
- Engagement was low in all but two classes.
- As long as students were not disruptive, they were allowed to sit quietly and not engage in learning at all.
- Teachers needed support in lesson design and execution.
- Some teachers struggled with classroom management.
- The learning was disconnected from my student's lived experiences.

The data I collected and the patterns that emerged from this shadow experience helped drive the professional development (PD) that we planned for teachers. The PD that we provided became more relevant to the teachers because we were not simply basing our PD focus on numbers from a spreadsheet. We were triangulating assessment data, grades, and what we observed from classroom visits, particularly these shadow days (the entire leadership team had to perform one). Our conversations about student performance and teacher needs were so much richer because they came from living, breathing experiences not simply observational snapshots or uncontextualized data.

Culturally Responsive Practice #2: Hire Teachers of Color

If you want to establish a more culturally responsive school you have to hire more teachers of color. Students need to see people who look like them teaching and leading. Research shows that African American students benefit from having African American teachers (Gershenson et al., 2017; Milner, 2006). These teachers are more likely to have high expectations of them, provide requisite support, recommend them for Honors and AP classes and are less likely to recommend them for suspension or expulsion. Similar research reveals that all students (yes, even white students) benefit from being taught by and attending schools led by people of color. One of the best ways to combat long-held notions of African American and Latinx inferiority and racism is to surround children with living examples of excellence. Racism thrives in racial isolation. When people from diverse backgrounds converge and establish community with each other, it is difficult if not impossible to hold on to stereotypes and tropes. When we begin to normalize people of color in positions of authority and power in our schools, students are better equipped to reject racism and xenophobia. Yes, African Americans can be outstanding basketball players, but they can make great chemistry and English teachers too. Yes, Asians make great doctors, but they make great history teachers too.

If you are a principal, be mindful of surrendering your hiring responsibilities to teacher committees. Despite student needs, teachers are more likely to prefer and recommend candidates they have a personal and cultural connection with. They are more comfortable with candidates that look like them, speak like them, and that they share experiences with. Subconsciously, and despite what the job description may indicate, they seek candidates that they can be friends with.

Culturally Responsive Practice #3: Grow Your Own Staff

Schools with a commitment to cultural responsiveness do not make statements like "We are looking for African American and Latinx teachers, but they are not out there." Yes, there are challenges to finding teacher candidates of color. Many of these challenges are a result of systemic barriers that we will not delve into here. We know that this is a problem, however, a potential solution to the problem of finding candidates of color is to grow your own. If you have staff members of color who are dynamic teacher assistants, school assistants, or security staff, encourage them to go into teaching. This is a long-term strategy that will certainly pay off. These staff members often have positive relationships with some of your most challenging students and families. They are often connected to the community and have the ability to serve as both school employee and community ambassador. Already a school employee? Check. Great with kids? Check. Good with families? Check. Lives in and has deep connections to the community? Check. Sounds like this person would make a great teacher. Because of teacher shortages, many education programs have alternative certification pathways. Partner with your local colleges and universities. Host alternative certification classes in your school or district and grow your own staff. Everyone wins when you do this.

Culturally Responsive Practice #4: Empower Teachers and Staff of Color

Within schools that serve "diverse" communities there often exists a racialized hierarchy. Administrators are usually white, and the support staff, that is, disciplinarians, teacher assistants, lunchroom staff, and custodians are people of color. In predominantly white schools where there is an emerging African American population, often the security team is mostly, if not all, African American. One can easily see the problem with such a hierarchy and focusing on hiring teachers of color (see above) can disrupt such hierarchies. However, one way schools can be more culturally responsive institutions is to empower the voices of staff members who are just as much a part of the academic experience of students as administrators and teachers. Representatives of these support teams should be a part of the school leadership team and should be empowered to offer their expertise, and perspectives on how we can better serve the needs of all students. Support staff are often your front line when interacting with parents and often have relationships with some of your most challenging students. Amplify their voices. Just because they do not have a teaching license or a bachelor's degree does not mean that they cannot offer an important perspective.

Culturally Responsive Practice #5: Engage in Community Walks

"What are y'all marching for bruh?" This question was posed to me by a member of my school community during our first community walk. His curiosity was sparked seeing upward of forty teachers and staff members walking through the neighborhood one late summer morning. While he was unsure of the walk's purpose, we were clear it was to get to know the community. Whether we are comfortable admitting it or not, most people look at the African American and Latinx communities from a deficit perspective. Because of how we have been socialized and maybe even what we have seen, we enter predominantly African American communities fearful of being robbed, shot, or worse. What is not often acknowledged is that even in the poorest, most crime-ridden communities, there are tremendous assets and rich histories that must be seen and honored. When I was selected to serve as turnaround principal of the Sherman School of Excellence on Chicago's South Side, I knew that my greatest challenge would be assembling a team of teachers and staff who were not scared of the African American children and families we signed on to serve. Everything you heard about this particular neighborhood was negative. This community, like so many predominantly African American neighborhoods nationally, struggled with poverty, gangs, drugs, and dysfunctional schools. Despite this reality, there were also dedicated and committed community warriors who fought daily to build a better life not just for their children but for others as well. I needed my staff to meet some of these people and the institutions that they were a part of. I needed them to understand that there was brilliance in this community and that it was not the hopeless, downtrodden place that most people thought it was. Rather than invite these community representatives into our school, we stepped away from the comfort of our school building and visited with members of the community on their turf and what we discovered was remarkable. This neighborhood, despite what we had heard on the news, read in the newspaper, or seen or social media had valuable assets. A beautiful park, long-standing restaurants, community organizations dedicated to combating violence and poverty, mom-and-pop grocery stores, day care centers, and homeless and battered women's shelters all existed within this "hopeless" neighborhood. This became another powerful learning experience for both our teachers and staff, regardless of color or years of experience. We learned that the community our students came from while challenging, was a community of fighters and survivors. And while much was needed to help transform the community, people were not sitting by passively waiting for Superman; they were taking an active role in reshaping their own lives. We learned there were resources in this community that we could leverage to help us do our jobs better. But most importantly, we learned that we were not the smartest people in the community and that there were institutions in the neighborhood that we could rely on—expertise we could request to better serve our students.

Culturally Responsive Practice #6: Prioritize Being in Classes

I have always thought that the best part of being a school leader is having full unadulterated access to the entire schoolhouse. You have a backstage pass to every classroom, gym, cafeteria, and office. As principal, I would start each day visiting every classroom for at least a few minutes. I enjoyed checking in with my teachers, staff and students, it was my daily routine. As a former high school teacher, I really wanted to get a feel for how elementary school classrooms operated. When I became CAO, I prioritized being in classrooms because I was engaging in organizational diagnosis. In short, classroom visits were a tremendous source of learning for me. Classrooms were also where the magic was happening. Culturally responsive educators understand that whether you are a principal, assistant principal, or department chair, you must prioritize being in classrooms not just to evaluate teachers. While that may be part of the job, your first priority is to learn what is happening in classrooms so that you have a better sense of the student experience and the ways you need to support your teachers moving forward. Teachers pay attention to what you pay attention to. It does not matter what you say, it really only matters what you do.

Culturally responsive educators prioritize spending time where students spend the majority of their time and that is in classrooms. The provision of feedback and coaching is a major responsibility of culturally responsive educators. Developing teacher capacity to craft and execute high quality lessons that enhance the academic experience of students is imperative. Deep instructional leadership work cannot happen in the office. It only happens when school leaders, principals in particular, prioritize being in classrooms and observing instruction.

Culturally Responsive Practice #7: Counsel Out Bad Teachers and Staff

Somewhere between 90% and 95% of teachers and staff want to do what is right by children. The other 5% to 10% are what I call "kid killers." These are adults who need to find another profession. Because we prioritize adult comfort over student needs, we allow these individuals to continue to harm children. These are the adults who, no matter how much support you give, how much coaching and mentoring you invest in them, have made it clear that they have no intention of making any effort to improve their practices. They blame kids, take no accountability for their actions, and are unwilling to do what is necessary to support their students. They use colorless but racist language, long for the good old days, and suck all the positive energy out of the room. These people need to go. Being willing to counsel out bad teachers and staff requires two things: familiarity with your district's collective bargaining agreement (we do not want to violate contractual rights) and courage.

Becoming a more culturally responsive educator requires more than simply a set of strategies, it requires a commitment to changing how we enact our roles and responsibilities. It requires a shift in mindset, it requires us to be willing to step outside of our comfort to forge deeper relationships with our students and our families. Consider the seven culturally relevant practices in this chapter—How might you implement them in your school tomorrow? What other culturally relevant practices would you like to incorporate into your current practices?

CHAPTER 2 SUMMARY

- All schools are culturally responsive, but not every culture that is represented in a school is appropriately responded to.

- Creating a Culture of C.A.R.E. requires adults to create educational spaces that acknowledge, respond to, and celebrate the diversity of students' cultures in meaningful ways and offer full and equitable access to education for all students.

- Culturally responsive educators see cultural diversity as an asset and a way to build students' cultural competence and awareness.

- Cultural responsiveness requires courage and the willingness to step outside one's comfort zone to meet the needs of oft-marginalized students.

- All students benefit from culturally responsive spaces, not just African American and Latinx students.

REFLECTION QUESTIONS

1. Why is it important to create culturally responsive educational spaces? How do you envision your students and families benefiting from a culturally responsive school?

2. How has your school been hostile to marginalized students? What are you currently doing to address hostility and repair the harm caused to students?

3. What might your families and students say about your school's responsiveness to their needs if asked?

4. How do you ensure that students, particularly your most marginalized students have access to the fullness of the school experience?

5. What actions can you take tomorrow to create a more culturally responsive school environment?

The "A": Affirmation

LEARNING GOALS

As a result of reading this chapter, educators will:

☐ Understand the importance of creating and sustaining culturally and identity-affirming spaces for students.

☐ Be able to gauge whether their students feel affirmed or not.

☐ Be able to implement strategies that affirm the identities of their students.

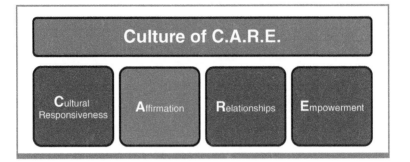

WHAT IS AFFIRMATION?

Affirmation is the act or process of affirming something or giving a heightened sense of value, typically through the experience of something emotionally or spiritually uplifting. There is an emerging body of literature on the importance of affirmation in schools. Two types of affirming environments have risen to the forefront of the debate: *culturally affirming* classrooms/schools and *identity-affirming* classrooms/schools (Allen et al., 2013; Buchanan-Rivera, 2022). Before launching into a short description of each, please reflect on the following questions:

1. What is your cultural identity (think: nationality, language, ethnicity, race, religion)? What or who do you feel connected to culturally and why?

2. What other identities do you bring to your work that shape who you are as an educator (think: social class, education, gender, sexual orientation, age, mental or physical ability, income)?

3. How do you acknowledge and celebrate your cultural identity(ies)?

4. Are you aware of the distinct cultural identities that are present within your school and classroom?

5. How do you acknowledge or celebrate cultural diversity in your school and classroom?

We start with these five reflection questions because a prerequisite to affirming others is ensuring that we are in tune with and have a deep understanding of the identities that shape who we are and how our identities influence what we believe, what we think, and how we act.

Cultural identity refers to who our students identify with or belong to, with a particular emphasis on their nationality, ethnicity, race, gender, and religion. Culturally affirming spaces affirm the cultural identities of the students and the adults within them. Culturally affirming adults view cultural diversity as a mechanism to enhance the academic experiences of students. These assets are used as tools to build cultural competence, understanding, awareness, and to create a sense of belonging.

Educators in culturally affirming schools and classrooms reject notions of color blindness and work incessantly to establish and sustain mutually respectful environments, where students are respectful of other students, adults show respect to students, and students are respectful to adults. In these environments, students' emotional, intellectual, and physical safety are prioritized. Culturally affirming spaces protect people from the microaggressions that are often present in schools and classrooms, whereby our most marginalized students are victims of insensitivity, hostility, stereotyping, insults, and invisibility (Allen et al., 2013).

Whereas a culturally affirming space centers a student's cultural identity, identity affirming spaces acknowledge and celebrate the full humanity and dignity of students, including their racial, ethnic, language, gender, sexual, and other elements of their multifaceted identities such as visible and invisible disabilities. The educator in the identity affirming space embraces the varied identities of their students and recognizes how those identities shape not just who they are but how they interact with the world, and most importantly how the world interacts with them and shapes how they feel about themselves. In *Identity Affirming Classrooms; Spaces that Center Humanity*, Erica Buchanan-Rivera (2022) argues, "an identity affirming classroom is a student-centered environment where the contributions, reflections, and feedback from youth are celebrated and encouraged" (p. 142). The implication here is that an educator must first be willing to surrender control of the classroom to create a student-centered space where students are the drivers of the learning experience. This means that the curricula, the lesson designs, and the learning tasks that students engage in are driven by student interests, student learning needs, and by prior learning experiences of students. Students must see themselves in the curricular materials. Additionally, the histories and contributions of individuals and groups they share identity with must be represented and the students' lived experiences must be validated.

Both conceptualizations have value. Culturally affirming spaces center on a student's cultural identity, while identity-affirming spaces center on the multifaceted and varied identities that are representative of their full humanity. Educators should strive to provide for both. Within the context of the C.A.R.E. Framework, the "Affirmation" pillar is best examined by reflecting on one essential question: Do students feel good about who they are when they are in your classroom or your school?

> **Do students feel good about who they are when they are in your classroom or your school?**

We can debate the merits of cultural and identity affirmation but essentially, building a school culture that affirms students requires a deep commitment to making students feel good about who they are and about who and what they are striving to be. Unfortunately, for so many students, schools are hostile places (see Chapter 2) where they are othered, and made to feel bad about themselves, and their families. Affirming students in schools requires that educators celebrate, honor, protect, and cultivate their identities. It requires that adults in schools nurture, love, and value the uniqueness of students and validate their sense of self. It requires that we care for our students enough that we offer emotional support and encouragement.

It requires that educators honor who the student is and not devalue them because they are not who they want them to be. A child who is affirmed is a child who feels good about who they are.

Educators who are committed to creating an affirming school environment know that there is really only one way to determine whether the school is successful in making children feel good about themselves: They ask them. School leaders, teachers, and staff might be surprised at the amount of students who feel isolated and disconnected from the larger school community and the only way to determine the quality of your students' relationship to the school is to ask the students themselves. Below are ten questions educators can ask to ascertain whether students feel affirmed at school. There is no "right' way to utilize these questions. A teacher, for example, can survey students using these questions at the beginning of the school year as part of an introductory activity. Using these questions, school leaders can survey all age-appropriate students. Leaders may also decide to use these questions as part of focus groups to examine the experiences of specific groups of students.

DO CHILDREN IN YOUR SCHOOL FEEL GOOD ABOUT THEMSELVES?

Ask them. . .

1. Do you feel like you belong in your school?

2. Do you feel like you belong in your classroom?

3. When was the last time an adult said something nice to you? How often do adults say nice things to you?

4. Do you feel important at school or in your classroom?

5. Do you feel cared for at school or in your classroom?

(Continued)

(Continued)

6. When was the last time you were celebrated for something you did?

7. Do you feel like your teacher knows who you are?

8. Do the adults in this school acknowledge you by saying good morning, or speaking to you in the hallway?

9. Does your teacher show concern when you are absent from school?

10. Is there one adult in school you trust to go to if you need help?

[you might consider including questions for educators ... something like...]

1. Which children do you feel belong in your school?

2. Which children do you feel don't belong?

3. Are there children who don't feel like they belong in your school? Who are they? Why do you think they feel that way?

4. What daily actions do you take to make sure children feel a sense of belonging?

5. Did you say something nice to each children in your class today?

6. How do you make children feel important?

7. How do you make children feel cared for?

8. How do you celebrate students' accomplishments? Do you find something to celebrate in each child?

9. Do you know each of your students personally?

10. Do you greet students in the hallway and engage them in conversations?

11. How do you show concern for students who were absent?

12. How do you invite students to participate?

Student responses to these questions are educative for any teacher or school leader interested in learning more about how their students are experiencing school. By asking these questions educators demonstrate an interest in and a willingness to protect students' well-being. The questions remove speculation and assumptions about how students are feeling and give student's authority to use their voices to communicate their feelings and experiences.

> The child who is not embraced by the village will burn it down to feel its warmth.
>
> **—African Proverb**

In public schools across the nation, there are significant numbers of students who do not feel embraced by their schools, their teachers, or their administrators. They have been made to feel less than. Nowadays, we often refer to these children as *marginalized*; before we just did not see them. They make up a large swath of our student population but we do not always fully acknowledge their existence. These are the students whose cultural and ethnic identities were not acknowledged. These are students who could not access the full depth and breadth of the academic experience because of language barriers. These are the students who rarely if ever participate in enrichment or extracurricular activities. They attend our schools under the cloak of invisibility only to be seen if they violate a school rule or policy. These unseen students whose identities are not affirmed lack a sense of belonging to the school. They do not see themselves in the curriculum, they often do not view their school lessons as connected to their lives, and often they are taught by educators whom they do not share a cultural identity or connection with. As mentioned earlier, school enrollment data reveal that the majority of children who attend public schools in the United States identify as Latinx, African American, Asian, indigenous, or mixed race, yet close to 80% of teachers are white women and the majority of principals are white men (nearly 80%) (National Center for Education Statistics, 2023). America's public school teachers and leaders look very different from its student population. The stark cultural differences between educators and students and the lack of representation in school leadership and within the teaching ranks often create significant student challenges. Racialized achievement disparities, overly punitive disciplinary policies and practices, and acute disproportionality are just a few indicators that point to schools being hostile places for students, particularly those who come from historically marginalized communities (Khalifa, 2016). Yet they are mandated to attend these schools every day. They are blamed for failure, but the conditions that perpetuate their failure and disengagement from school are rarely examined. African American boys, for example, are often the target of these hostile learning environments. Most are aware that the dropout rate of African American males is nearly 8% nationally, but most are unaware that many of these same males have been systematically pushed out of school since pre-kindergarten, where they represent 50% of the children suspended or expelled but only 20% of those enrolled (Williford et al., 2023). As these students matriculate through the educational system they are often labeled as "problem kids" and because of their hypervisibility or in some cases invisibility they engage in behaviors that seriously disrupt our school cultures. They begin to burn the village down. They burn it down not because they are evil or bad; they burn it down because disruptive and undesirable behavior is the only way they know how to communicate their needs to a system that was not designed to be attentive to their needs or to support their development.

How unfortunate that so many children are legally required to attend schools that do not make them feel good about themselves. It should be no surprise that so many students struggle with self-esteem issues, depression, disengagement, and a lack of motivation. The pandemic revealed what most already knew: Schools were not serving the needs of all of their students, and tragically despite all the rhetoric calling for a "reimagination" of schools, most schools have reverted to the same behaviors and practices that existed prepandemic. These practices have effectively worked to push students out of school and even those who attend school regularly are "quiet quitting" school. The common response to the realities of academic underperformance, disproportionality, and disengagement has been to launch an equity campaign. One would be hard-pressed to find a school or district that has not (at least in theory) made a commitment to educational equity. Expertly crafted equity statements and policies appear on most school and district websites. Most schools and districts have equity teams and ambassadors, and many more have invested tens of thousands of dollars retaining consulting teams who have promised to help root out the inequities that exist in these schools.

Oftentimes the equity work focuses on addressing student results. In many districts, there are stark contrasts in how white students perform versus African American and Latinx students. With good intentions, these achievement disparities compel schools and districts to employ intervention strategies designed to "fix" the underperforming students. The heightened focus on results and outcomes often perpetuates greater inequities, because the root cause of the subpar student performance is not examined. How do we expect students to perform in spaces where they do not feel affirmed?

STUDENT CREED
by Chike Akua

I am a student seeking to be a scholar.

The standard is excellence today and tomorrow.

I am disciplined, focused, and on time.

I am organized, respectful, and responsible.

I am on a mission to elevate myself, my family, my community, and humanity.

Source: Used with permission.

This student creed written by Chike Akua was recited every morning by Sherman School of Excellence students on Chicago's southside, a school I led back in 2006. Sherman was a unique place. Prior to the school being "turned around," it was labeled a "failing" school. Standardized test data revealed that less than 25% of students met state standards in Reading or Mathematics (CPS Accountability Report, 2005). The narrative was that the students were failing and therefore the school needed to be "turned around." Under the turnaround model all the adults in the school were fired or reassigned but the children were allowed to stay. While this methodology was deemed the least disruptive of all school reform options, what was overlooked, ignored, or miscalculated was the impact that this decision would have on the identities, the psyche, and the self-esteem of Sherman students. They were students at a failing school, and because of that narrative, many saw themselves as failing students. This, coupled with the reality that everything and everyone that they once knew about their school was gone with the stroke of a pen, shook many students to the core. In working to rebuild the academic confidence and self-esteem of students, the leaders of Sherman School of Excellence adopted Akua's Student Creed to initiate the gradual reprogramming of the subconscious minds of the students to help them realize that they were not failures. The daily recitation of this creed helped them see themselves not as failing students in a once-failing school but as disciplined scholars capable of excellence. This creed encouraged students to think better of themselves but also communicated that the adults understood the greatness that they were capable of and the standard that they were going to be held to.

CONCRETE PRACTICES FOR OPERATIONALIZING AFFIRMATION

This section aims to present practical, research-informed strategies to ensure teachers are affirming the identities and acknowledging the humanity in every child they encounter. The pressures of social media, the stresses associated with the pandemic, and an ever-divisive world require educators to intentionally elevate the self-esteem and self-worth of the students they serve. So many students, particularly African

American, Latinx, and poor students, are made to feel inferior, effectively souring their academic experiences and pushing them away from school.

Affirming Practice #1: Begin Each Day With the Recitation of a Positive Affirmation or Creed

In the Sherman School of Excellence example, students recited the same creed daily: "I am a student seeking to be a scholar . . . I am disciplined, focused, and on time." The recitation of positive affirmations can have a significant impact on a student's self-worth, and cognitive science supports this (Cascio et al., 2015). Neuroplasticity refers to the brain's ability to adapt, restructure and rewire after exposure to certain stimuli. Traumatic brain injuries often result in the loss of the ability to speak or perform certain functions; however, the brain can relearn these abilities through exposure to specific stimuli as part of rehabilitation and therapy. These stimuli effectively work to repair or create new neural pathways. Positive affirmations are the stimuli that have the potential to repair or create new neural pathways for our students. While students may not be suffering from the results of a traumatic brain injury, many are suffering from the trauma of micro-aggressions and isolation in schools. Just as the Sherman students were suffering from being associated with a failing school, other students are suffering from being labeled and treated as deviant, lazy, or troublesome. Studies have proven that positive affirmations help activate parts of the brain associated with reward. Students who are bombarded with microaggressions (such as those who have their names constantly mispronounced, are frequently corrected for not using "good English," and those who are forced to represent the perspectives of an entire race or class of people), and who feel isolated and othered might never have these reward centers activated in school. This lack of activation causes fear, anxiety, and depression leading to disengagement. The recitation of positive student affirmations or creeds can effectively combat these negative feelings leading to a happier, more fulfilled, and more engaged student.

Affirming Practice #2: Pronounce Names . . . Correctly

If you are committed to sustaining an affirming environment for your students, you must commit to pronouncing their names correctly. Name shaming or constantly mispronouncing your students' names is a microaggressive behavior that communicates a lack of respect for students' language, culture, family, and community. Ask for help when trying to pronounce a student's name, and spell it phonetically so you can get it right. Making an effort makes all the difference when affirming a student's identity. Please do not believe it is right to shorten or give a student a nickname simply because you do not want to put in the effort to pronounce the name correctly.

Affirming Practice #3: I See You!

In urban parlance, when someone says "I see you," they are saying they are impressed by you and that they understand you and where you are coming from. Affirming a student requires that educators work to get to know their students not just as vessels to deposit knowledge and skills into but as human beings. It requires that we "see" our students—that we understand who they are and where they are coming from. Who are they outside of the classroom? Outside of school? How do they see themselves? Where is their family from? What languages are spoken in the home? What identities are most important to them? These are all questions that allow us to know our students better. Having individual conversations with every student is the best but probably not the most realistic way for a teacher or administrator to learn about their students, so I would suggest two strategies that are equally effective and less time-consuming. The first is the identity wheel activity. You can easily download an identity wheel from the internet or create your own. The wheel provides identities that students can choose from to describe how they see themselves and select the identities that are most important to them. It might include identities such as race, ethnicity, native language, gender, birth order, religion, age, and ability status (i.e., are they living with some sort of disability). Having students reflect and share their responses to these identity exercises help foster an environment where students feel seen and validated. While the complexity of the language may need to be adjusted or modified, you can use the identity wheel activity with most grade levels of students. Educators can model vulnerability to students by completing an identity wheel and sharing it with students. Another way to get to know students is by having them complete a student information sheet. The document includes a list of prompts and questions that students respond to that help provide a comprehensive picture of who they are. You might ask questions such as "What adjectives best describe who you are? How do you learn best? What do you love about yourself? About school? These questions help educators learn much more about their students and can be done on the first day or across the first week of school. Schools can commit to posting student identity wheels or excerpts of student information sheets (with students' permission first) in common areas around the school so that everyone can have an opportunity to get to know each other and foster greater connectivity within the school community.

Affirming Practice #4: Leverage Affirming Language and Behaviors When Interacting With Students

If affirming students is about making them feel good about themselves and making them feel loved, respected, and appreciated for who they are, then educators must commit to leveraging affirming language and behaviors with students. There is a saying that "What's in the heart has a way of seeping out." If the educator's heart is filled with negativity, doubt, and stereotypical thoughts about their students, those feelings will seep out. Affirming educators engage in behaviors to affirm and uplift their students' sense of belonging and value. They greet their students outside the school or classroom each morning and make all students feel welcome. You would be surprised at how often students complain about their teachers not greeting them in the morning. I have worked in historically marginalized communities for much of my career and I say, without hyperbole, that for so many students, simply making it to school is a miracle. Students overcome seemingly insurmountable obstacles to come to school. Many have to traverse gang territories and crime-ridden neighborhoods, and long bus rides, and manage a multitude of adult responsibilities but when they arrive at school, they do not get a pat on the back or a certificate for their persistence. Instead, they are often scolded for being a few minutes late. Rather than scold students for being late, educators should celebrate the fact that the student wanted to attend school enough that they pushed through adversity and then work with the student and the family to ensure that the barriers to them arriving to school on time are addressed. It may require, for example, that the student's schedule be adjusted to a later start time to accommodate for challenges that the student might be experiencing in the morning. It might require leaders to adjust the master schedule. There are schools that officially start the school day at 8 a.m., but do not start instructional time to 8:15 a.m. or 8:30 a.m. The additional 15–30 minutes of cushion allows extra time in the morning for teachers to get their classrooms settled, to ensure that students have eaten breakfast and to reduce the amount of actual instructional time that students miss due to issues of tardiness that are beyond the student's control. Affirming educators acknowledge students' lived experiences and reward them by saying, "It's great seeing you today."; "I'm glad you are here."; "I'm impressed that despite everything you are going through, you came to class." (just as a reminder, educators must get to know their students before they even realize that these types of affirming comments are warranted). Affirming educators also find reasons to compliment students appropriately. Complimenting students in appropriate ways makes students feel seen. Complimenting a student or acknowledging a new hairstyle, haircut, or a new shirt could make all the difference in how a student sees themselves and how they view their teacher or the adults in their school.

Affirming Practice #5: Effort Optimism

One of the most heartbreaking realities of many students' experiences is that they rarely receive any positive feedback from their teachers or other adults they interact with. These are students that are often labeled as "bad kids" or "frequent fliers." They seldom if ever are made to feel welcome. These students who may have been labeled as bad or deviant as early as pre-K or kindergarten have constantly found themselves on the fringes of the schools they attend. They may attend school every day but spend each day disengaged in the back of the classroom, in and out of the dean's or principal's office, and are often barred from recess, field trips, and other enrichment activities. These students begin to adopt the identity that has been constructed for them. They have been labeled *trouble-makers* and *deviants* so they adopt the identity of trouble-makers and deviants. The provision of positive feedback is motivating and encouraging and has a tremendous impact on the development of a student's self-concept. Even the most challenging students will respond to genuine and authentic feedback. The recognition of specific actions and positive narration of those actions will compel the student to engage in similar behaviors. Even if the student is not meeting the standard or the expectation exactly as it has been set, acknowledging the growth and the progress that a student is making is important. When a student who rarely turns in homework, finally submits an assignment, celebrate the student and appreciate the progress. Celebrate a student who arrives at school or class on time after being late the previous two weeks.

At Urban Prep Academies in Chicago, a network of schools that served African American males exclusively and where I served as chief academic officer, students met in the gymnasium each morning for Community. The leaders of Urban Prep were committed to finding reasons to celebrate the young men they served. They knew it was necessary to affirm young men from the south and west sides of Chicago who were more likely to be murdered, commit suicide, or go to prison than graduate from college. Creating an affirming educational environment for these young men was essential to reshaping their academic identities and constructing a positive self-concept. Knowing this, Urban Prep leaders used Community to celebrate these young men for a variety of feats and accomplishments, academic, athletic, citizenship, and effort. Appreciating the effort that these young men put into becoming better students and better young men made them try harder. These celebrations fueled what Teresa Perry calls "effort optimism," which is the belief that their hard work will yield benefits (Perry et al., 2003). Every school has a code of conduct, a discipline manual, and a plan for how to punish students for disruptive or undesirable behavior; very few, if any, have a systematic approach to providing positive feedback to their students or ways to celebrate their successes.

Affirming Practice #6: Call or Write Home With Good News; Share the Good and Uplift the Child

There is good in every child. For a variety of reasons, educators do not often have the opportunity to share that good with the child and their family. There are few things more important in affirming and elevating the self-worth of a child than calling home or sending home a letter with good news. Taking just a few minutes out of each day or week to call or write to a parent or guardian with good news, to offer a compliment, or to celebrate something good that a student has done makes that child and parent feel good about themselves and motivates them to continue to engage in positive behaviors. This can be easily done using a call or note log. Leaders and teachers can commit to calling or sending home short notes to a specific number of families, designating what good news they are going to share and cycling through their logs to ensure that every family is contacted at least once in a given cycle. Doing this will dramatically change the relationship the educator has with the student and their family and the school at large. As a principal, I recall inviting a parent into my office to share some good news about their child and to express appreciation to the parent for all the support they were giving the student who was experiencing some challenges in school. I wanted the parent to know that despite these challenges, we were not giving up on the child and that we were proud of the progress we were observing. Initially silent as I spoke, they broke down into tears, expressing appreciation for sharing that feedback. This parent went from an angry and often confrontational parent to one of our major allies and supporters in large part due to our ten-minute conversation.

Creating and sustaining an affirming school environment is essential for all students but has particular benefits for historically marginalized students. Every student should feel good about who they are. Few adults would choose to be an adolescent or teenager today because of the pressures that youth today have to face. Social media, the threat of school shootings, unrealistic academic pressures, and highly competitive school environments make students increasingly miserable. Unless educators are intentional about creating a counterculture that nurtures, loves on, and values the uniqueness of every child, our students will continue to struggle with feelings of isolation, apathy, dejection, and depression. Affirming a child requires that we go above and beyond to ensure that every child feels good about themselves, who they are, and who they are striving to be.

VIGNETTES OF AFFIRMATION IN PRACTICE

The Rolodex

Mr. Beamon, veteran principal of a mid-size elementary school understood the importance of affirming students. He was very deliberate about making students feel seen. Each school year, he would have his clerical staff affix the picture of every student in the school to a notecard. Notecards included the student's name, grade, classroom, and space for Mr. Beamon to jot down personal notes about each child. These notes came from what he observed, information he learned about the child from conferences,

(Continued)

(Continued)

and updates shared by teachers. Each day, Mr. Beamon would randomly select three to five students that he would approach in the lunchroom or in the hallways to ask them about their day, or to ask about a specific update of which he was aware. These short but impactful conversations with students helped him to learn more about his students but more importantly, it made students feel seen and affirmed. Imagine being a student, and **the principal** approached you with a question about your new cat, or about the new house you moved in? Or if he pulled you aside and said great game last night or said "Hey I heard you did a great job on your project in Mrs. Jones' class."? The "Rolodex" was a mechanism that allowed Mr. Beamon to continuously interact with students in authentic and genuine ways and allowed him to regularly affirm students who might otherwise go unseen.

Get to Know Me

The hallways of Tubman High School are adorned with "Get to Know Me" posters. The posters include a student photo and five unique facts about each student (favorites, interests outside of school, college or career aspirations and important identities). Each quarter, a grade level is highlighted. While posters are up, students, teachers, and staff are encouraged to read the posters and place sticky notes of appreciation, compliments, and the ways they connect with the student being profiled. Student leaders are charged with monitoring the activity on the posters ensuring that every student has affirming sticky notes placed upon it. This quarterly activity helps to foster a community of connectivity and belonging and it encourages students to practice being kind to one another.

Positive Bombardment

Adults in schools need to be affirmed too. At Chavez High School, a school that serves two thousand students and employs two hundred adults, Principal Juarez has worked incessantly to give this rather large high school a small school feel. To do so, she and the division heads employ a strategy called "positive bombardment." At the beginning of at least one of their division meetings per month, three teachers are randomly chosen to be bombarded with positivity. One by one, each of the three teachers are paraded to the center of the room, where they are instructed to close their eyes. Once their eyes are closed, they are bombarded with positive praise from colleagues for two full minutes. Praise ranges from, "I really like those shoes you wore last week" to "Students could not stop talking about how much fun the Columbus trial was in your class." Teachers are often brought to tears by the comments that they hear over the course of the two minutes and are genuinely surprised by what their colleagues share. While no one is forced to participate, most do because positivity is contagious and who does not want to be the subject of positive bombardment?

Rose Ceremony

Dr. Abdullah begins each quarterly staff meeting with a Rose Ceremony. As the principal of a large comprehensive high school, with over 175 teachers and staff members, it's important that she commits to building connectivity and community amongst staff. The day before each meeting she purchases a dozen roses, spreads them across the table at the front of the auditorium and invites teachers and staff members to grab and present a rose to a colleague. During rose

(Continued)

(Continued)

presentations, staff expresses gratitude and appreciation to their colleagues for support and acknowledge the achievements that might otherwise go unnoticed.

Both Positive Bombardment and the Rose Ceremony are ways to systemize the affirmation of adults. Adults who are affirmed and seen by their leaders and colleagues are more fulfilled at work, that fulfillment leads to happiness. Affirmed adults are more likely to affirm students and it only costs the price of a dozen roses and an investment of a few minutes before a meeting. Both strategies can be used with children as well.

CHAPTER 3 SUMMARY

- Affirmation is the act or process of affirming something, to give a heightened sense of value, typically through the experience of something emotionally or spiritually uplifting or showing emotional support and encouragement.

- Creating a Culture of C.A.R.E. requires adults to actively seek to make every child feel good about themselves. This is what it means to affirm a child.

- Culturally affirming spaces view cultural diversity and identity as assets rather than vulnerabilities.

- Identity-affirming spaces acknowledge and celebrate the full humanity and dignity of all students (and teachers) and their multifaceted identities.

- Educators should regularly ask themselves, "Do my students feel good about who they are when they are in my school or my classroom?"

REFLECTION QUESTIONS

1. How do you affirm students in your school?

2. Why do you think it is important to affirm children in your school?

3. Do students feel good about themselves in your school or classroom? How do you know?

4. What concrete strategies can you employ tomorrow to help students feel more affirmed in your school or classroom? What can you do long term?

5. Think about three to five students who you notice seem disconnected or disengaged from school. What are you committed to doing to increase their sense of belonging and engagement?

The "R": Relationships

LEARNING GOALS

As a result of reading this chapter, educators will:

☐ Understand the importance of establishing relationships with students.

☐ Be able to implement strategies that lead to establishing quality relationships with students.

Culture of C.A.R.E.			
Cultural Responsiveness	**A**ffirmation	**R**elationships	**E**mpowerment

What's in the heart has a way of seeping out.

In Chapters 2 and 3 of this book, I unpacked the first two pillars of the Culture of C.A.R.E. Framework: **C**ultural responsiveness and **A**ffirmation. I argued that a caring and nurturing school environment that promotes intellectual, social, emotional, and mental wellness must celebrate and respond to the cultural diversity and affirm the identities of its students. The "R" of the Culture of C.A.R.E. Framework represents "relationships." This is the pillar upon which the others rest. Educators cannot be culturally responsive, affirm the identities of students or empower them without the prioritization and establishment of positive relationships.

The Learning Seminar

Twenty years ago when I was a novice history teacher, I had an interaction with a veteran colleague. I was one of just a handful of African American teachers at a large comprehensive high school just outside of Chicago. At the time of my hiring, the district was working to examine the root causes of the achievement disparities that existed between African American students and their white peers. One of the recommendations borne from this work was the need for a mentoring program for African American boys. This program was called the "Learning Seminar." The seminar met daily at the end of the school day and I was charged with serving as their mentor, homework helper, advisor, and counselor. The district felt that a young six-foot six inch, two-hundred-and-fifty-pound idealistic teacher would be the perfect choice to lead this program. These were some of the toughest and most challenging young men in the school. They were what most schools call "frequent fliers." They were frequently involved in the disciplinary pipeline and often received poor grades usually due to noncompliance. These were the kind of students that would make some teachers question whether teaching was the **right** profession for them. I looked forward to seeing these young men each day. Despite what their GPAs indicated, these young men were intelligent, wise beyond their years, and talented in ways that are not always honored by schools. Over time, they became less like my students and more like my nephews or little brothers. A few months into the program, a teacher saw me talking to one of my Learning Seminar students in the hallway. He had gotten in trouble in another class and she overheard me lovingly admonishing him, instructing him to return to class, and informing him that we would revisit this conversation later. As he walked away, she approached me with a weird look of approval. She said to me, "These boys always listen to you and do not give you any trouble. It must be because you are so big." I was not sure what to say. First, she was wrong. Those boys drove me crazy half the time, but we needed each other. They needed my support and what I learned from them made me a better teacher. When they misbehaved or failed to turn in their homework or cut class, I felt it was an indictment on me and my mentorship. Second, and most importantly, they listened to me not because of fear but because of love. What she witnessed in that hallway was the manifestation of a positive relationship that I worked to form with that student and the rest of the young men in the Learning Seminar. I had proved to these young men, not with words, but through my actions, that I had their best interest in mind and that I was willing to do whatever it took to support them. Forging these relationships with this group of students meant I had to work to earn their trust, I had to be vulnerable, and most importantly I had to listen.

This chapter is divided into two parts. The first part is written for educators who do not yet see the value in investing in relationship-building. These are educators who do not realize how the lack of positive relationships with students undermines the efficacy of their teaching. In this section, my aim is to detail why relationships matter. The second part is written for those who believe that relationships matter but have not figured out how to establish relationships with their students. In this second section, I will share strategies to enhance the reader's capacity to establish high-quality relationships with their students.

WHY RELATIONSHIPS MATTER

Most educators agree that relationships matter. However, many students suffer because they do not have genuine and authentic relationships with their teachers and the other adults who help shape their academic experiences. As we discuss the necessity of building relationships it is important that we acknowledge that the responsibility for actively forging relationships with students is not shouldered by students alone. It is imperative that every adult in the school makes forming relationships with students a priority. In fact, it is likely that a student will interact with upward of three to five adults *before* starting their instructional day. The bus driver, crossing guard, or safe-passage worker is likely the first adult they encounter, followed by a security or safety officer, cafeteria worker, custodian, or an administrator. Imagine if these adults greeted each student they encountered warmly, inquired about the previous evening or their morning, performed a quick socioemotional check-in, and encouraged them to have a productive school day. Imagine the positive impact that would have on that child's psyche.

> No significant learning occurs without a significant relationship.
>
> **—Dr. James Comer (2001)**

Rich learning environments are characterized by a sense of community, belonging, humility, and openness. These attributes only exist in classrooms where there is mutual respect and trust between the teacher and their students. This does not happen without a meaningful relationship. Children who have had unfavorable academic experiences are more likely to distrust their teachers and schools in general. These feelings of distrust present as a lack of motivation and academic disengagement. The antidote lies in the establishment of positive relationships. When students feel an emotional and social connection with their teachers, they are more likely to engage in the educative process (Ladson-Billings, 1994). They will be more willing to take intellectual risks and more motivated to succeed in school. Establishing a positive relationship with students will lubricate the learning engine's gears and open the door for teachers to push them beyond their self-imposed academic limitations. Highly effective teachers know it is the investment in relationships, not the depositing of content knowledge or skills, that determines the potency of the learning experience. School leaders must require that their teachers be great stewards of instruction and keenly adept in establishing high quality relationships with all students. Educators rise to the level of the expectations of their leaders. If school leaders emphasize the importance of relationships, set the expectation that relationship-building is a pedagogical prerequisite and not an add-on, and model what effective relationship-building looks like, teachers will be more likely to prioritize it in their classrooms. The mistake that some leaders make, however, is creating an environment with a hyper-focus on student outcomes. The outcomes will take care of themselves if educators invest in establishing relationships.

> Kids don't learn from people they don't like.
>
> —**Rita Pierson (2013)**

If your students do not like you, they will not learn from you. It is really that simple. Teaching is not a popularity contest; however, it is in every educator's best interest to establish positive relationships with their students. Every teacher should want their students to say for example, "Mrs. Brown … yeah she's cool." When a student thinks that you are cool, what they are saying is that "I am willing to learn from you." "I will not do anything intentionally to get in the way of teaching and learning in the classroom and when I do, I will accept you redirecting me." Conversely, when a student dislikes or does not think their teacher is cool, they will become unmotivated and disengaged and their lack of motivation and engagement will present in disruptive ways.

Teachers who struggle with classroom management are often teachers who have not committed to establishing relationships with their students. These teachers have a mindset issue. They believe that the student is the sole beneficiary of the student–teacher relationship. They want their students to sit down, shut up, and learn—refusing to acknowledge that learning only happens when teacher and student relationship is fluid (meaning there are times when the teacher is the learner and times when the student is the teacher) (Ladson-Billings, 1994).

The fluidity of the student–teacher relationship provides fertile soil that enhances the growth and development of students. The veteran colleague that I referenced earlier did not understand that. In her opinion, students should view teachers as authority figures, and they should mindlessly comply with classroom and school rules and policies. She, as many teachers do, equated relationship-building with being too soft and losing control. Highly effective teachers understand that the best classroom management strategy is forming relationships with students. Students will play with and play for teachers they like. If your students like you when your principal conducts that formal observation, they will behave like angels. Why? Because they want you to look good. Why? Because they care about you. If they have no love for you they will let it be known how they feel about you. Ultimately, establishing positive relationships is in the best interest of the student, but teachers benefit as well. Teachers with great relationships with students have more fun and increased job satisfaction.

> Students don't care about your gradebook.
>
> —Dr. Lionel E. Allen, Jr. (that's me)

While serving as CAO of Urban Prep Academies in Chicago, I led the enactment of a no-zero policy. Urban Prep Academies is a 50l(c)(3) nonprofit organization that operates a network of all-boys public schools including the country's first charter high school for boys. The no-zero policy was our way of addressing vast inequities in grading and assessment practices. Its implementation sought to address the compliance-driven grading culture that existed in our schools and in doing so it moved us from an overreliance on punitive grading tactics to motivate our students (99% of whom were African American males) and shifted our focus to mastery and proficiency as indicators of student success. I will not launch into a discussion of the merits and inadequacies of the policy here, except to say that it was universally panned by teachers who viewed the policy as weak and overly progressive. They argued that the policy absolved students of responsibility for their grades and restricted teachers' ability to hold students accountable. The harsh reality is that many students are **not** motivated by grades. But they are motivated by the relationship they have with their teacher. They work for those to whom they feel connected. Weaponizing the grade book does not lead to improved student performance only strong relationships and good teaching can do that. As a result of the implementation of the no-zero policy, failure rates were reduced. Students revealed that before implementing the policy, their chances of passing some classes were ruined as early as the third or fourth week of the semester. But with the new policy students were able to benefit from improved performance.

CONCRETE PRACTICES FOR OPERATIONALIZING RELATIONSHIP-BUILDING

Whenever I am giving a talk or delivering a presentation, regardless of the topic, people want to jump right to strategies. Strategies are important. They allow us to actualize the theory. The strategies are the actions we take to address the dilemmas that live and breathe in our school. However, when it comes to the challenges that educators face in schools, strategies are rarely, if ever, enough. There is a saying "What's in the heart has a way of seeping out." When we think about serving our students, the strategies that we select to serve them are manifestations of how we think and feel about them. This is why typical school improvement efforts aimed at improving outcomes for African American, Latinx, and poor students are rooted in deficit-minded orientations. This means that educators already think less of these students so the strategies that they select often perpetuate the same inequities that the strategy was designed to address. When it comes to establishing relationships, educator mindset trumps strategy.

> Am I willing to invest the time, effort, and energy into establishing relationships with students with whom I have no cultural connection? Students who do not look like me, speak like me, and with whom I have few shared experiences?

If an educator does not answer that question with a resounding *yes*, then strategies will serve them no purpose.

It is also important to note that the enactment of one strategy is not enough to form a strong relationship with a student. Just as in a romantic relationship, the bond is formed through multiple small, but intentional actions over time. You must tend to the relationship and be attentive to it to grow it. When working with students, it starts with welcoming them to your class or school, smiling at them when you see them, asking about their lives outside of school, and showing care and concern when they seem down. It requires all these things and more, but it begins with how you feel about the student to begin with. If you long for the good ol' days when "kids respected adults" and the days "before the community changed," the students will sense that energy. Relationship-building starts with the adult seeking to form the relationship. The remainder of this section will detail practical strategies that educators can use to build relationships with their students.

Relationship-Building Practice #1: Emotional Emojis

Who doesn't love a good emoji? This strategy is a quick but effective way to gauge the energy of your classroom and open the door to establishing caring relationships with your students. Even in a classroom of twenty-five to thirty students, a teacher can rotate through this check-in efficiently. The teacher projects a set of emojis (see Figure 4.1) onto a screen giving students sixty seconds of reflection time to decide which emoji best represents how they feel. Then, the teacher calls on each student to share their emotional emoji representative. This is a terrific way to establish relationships with students and build classroom community. This is also a way to conduct a quick socioemotional check. Students will be

Figure 4.1 ◆ Emotional Emojis

excited   proud   angry   happy

scared   silly   disappointed   sick

confused   shy   loving   nervous

Source: istock.com/jsabiroya

reluctant to develop a relationship with a teacher who only cares about the content of their course or the topic of the lesson for the day. When you show students you care about them as human beings, they will be more motivated to learn from you. Think: Maslow before Bloom's.

Relationship-Building Practice #2: Two-Word Check-In

Similar to the Emotional Emoji activity, the Two-Word Check-In activity allows students to explore the complexity of their emotions. The teacher provides time for the students to reflect on and label how they feel. Students can produce the words on their own or the teacher might provide words for students to choose from (see Figures 4.2 and 4.3). After a minute or so, the students will take turns sharing their two words with the class.

Figure 4.2 ◆ Two-Word Check-In

Name:_____

Two Word Check In

tired   sad   overwhelmed

happy   excited   silly

confused   energetic   calm

bored   nervous   focused

I feel _____ and

_____.

Source: Catherine Ryan

Figure 4.3 ◆ Emotion and Feeling Wheel

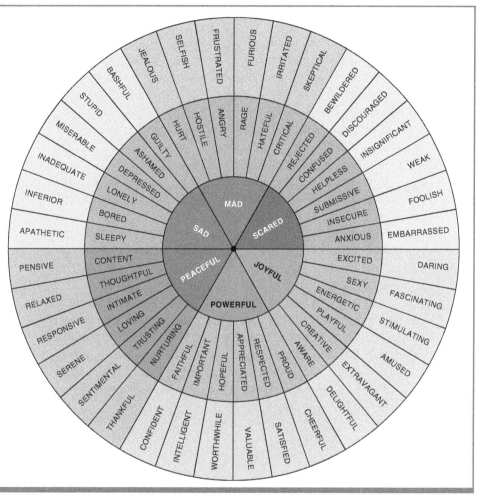

Source: Wilcox (1982)

Like the "Emotional Emoji" activity, the "Feelings Check-In" allows students to explore the complexity of their emotions. The teacher provides time for the students to reflect on and label how they feel. Students can produce the words on their own, or the teacher might provide words for students to choose from (see Figures 4.2 and 4.3). After a minute, the students will take turns sharing the words that best capture how they feel with the class. Students can be directed to choose two words that best capture how they feel (see Figure 4.2) or more, depending on whether the teacher wants students to engage in a deeper probing of feelings (see Figure 4.3). The value of this activity is in the exploration of emotional complexity (it is OK to grapple with competing or conflicting emotions), and it provides an opportunity for the teacher to model vulnerability and emotional awareness through their participation in the activity. It provides students with practice in expressing their feelings in a structured and productive way. The Feelings Wheel (See Figure 4.3) was not specifically designed with school-aged children in mind but can be used with students in intermediate grades and above; in fact, I have used this tool regularly in my graduate courses and professional development seminars with aspiring and in-service school leaders. In creating this important tool, Wilcox (1982) emphasizes the importance of emotional intelligence – the ability to recognize one's and other's emotions. Emotional intelligence is an important capacity to develop in students and the benefits are far-reaching both as an academic and SEL strategy. When children become adept at recognizing their own emotions, they are more apt to engage in emotional regulation, more readily capable of expressing compassion to others and developing self-compassion, which is so important in today's society when students are bombarded with messaging that makes them questions their value and worth (Wilcox, 1982).

TWO-WORD CHECK-IN

The value in this activity is the exploration of emotional complexity (it is OK to grapple with competing or conflicting emotions) and it provides an opportunity for the teacher to model vulnerability and emotional awareness. It gives students practice in expressing their feelings in a structured and productive way. Investment in this activity reminds students that the teachers care about how they feel and not just how smart they are. It also provides an opportunity for students to see the human side of the teacher which will help create greater connectivity between them.

Relationship-Building Practice #3: Just Listen

With all due respect, sometimes we need to just shut up and listen to our students. Teachers who value and understand the importance of establishing relationships know that one of the best strategies is to simply listen. This can be accomplished in a variety of ways. As a principal, I would greet students as they entered the school in the morning and engage them in small talk. "How are you doing?" "Are you having a good morning?" If they looked sad, down, or depressed, "What's wrong? Are you OK?" Asking questions about their caretakers, their siblings, or something you noticed about them (new haircut, presentation in class, something they were reading) goes a long way toward establishing strong relationships with students.

As a teacher, I engaged in informal conversations with students as they entered the classroom. Checking in on my students' well-being, greeting them with a smile, and asking them if they were OK was an essential part of how I started many of my classes. I also established formalized structures to create opportunities for students to express themselves and for me to listen. Elementary, middle, and high school teachers can start the year with activities that allow students to share who they are and what they are interested in outside of school. They can share their interests, their hobbies, television shows they watch, and extracurricular activities they participate in at school. This can be done using the "Who I Am" or "Getting to Know Me" Sheets (referenced in the "Affirmation" chapter). The activity can also be done verbally. This information can be used to identify similarities among students but also similarities with their teacher as well, as it allows educators to inquire about students' lives outside of the classroom. If a student, for example, shares that they have dance practice after school, I would ask questions about the type of dance they performed, how long they have been dancing, and when their next performance is. Simply expressing an interest in their life outside of school changes the relationship between you and that student.

As a history teacher, I would schedule what I called Current Events Day a few Fridays per month. During Current Events Day, students would bring in an article from a newspaper, magazine, or share something happening in their lives of interest to them. They completed a short summary and analysis of the article and we would spend the entire class period discussing what they wanted to discuss. I would listen to them. On those days, I was the student, and they were the teachers. I was often fascinated by our conversations and referenced them as I designed subsequent lessons. These were some of my most memorable days as a teacher.

Relationship-Building Practice #4: Engage With Them on Their Turf

All our students have talents that sometimes go unnoticed in our schools. If you are a school leader or teacher one of the best ways to form a relationship with a student is to go and watch them perform, compete, or work. It means a lot to students when their teachers and administrators show up to their games, their performances, or patronize the restaurant or the store where they work. Whenever we can engage with the whole child and learn about what they are interested in or responsible for, it makes us better able to enrich their learning. It also enables us to better support their needs. Our students are so much more than they show us in our classrooms and schools. When an educator makes an effort to step outside of *their* comfort zones and engage students where they are most comfortable, it opens a world of possibilities and serves as one small but mighty step toward strengthening that bond.

Ms. Brewer

Ms. Brewer was a middle school teacher at a mid-size elementary school on the south side of Chicago. She was a veteran teacher who was well respected by both her colleagues and had worked hard to connect with students. This school year was different as she struggled to bond with about three students in her middle school science class. These students had become increasingly difficult to manage in the class and were becoming disruptive. Frustrated and concerned about what to do, she approached her assistant principal, Ms. Abdul, for suggestions. As the assistant principal and disciplinarian, she had forged tight bonds with the "frequent fliers" and their families. Seeing Ms. Brewer's frustration, Ms. Abdul quickly suggested that she invite those students to have lunch with her. After initially being stunned at the suggestion, Ms. Brewer accepted the advice and invited each of the three students to lunch. She asked them what they wanted for lunch, had it delivered, and they broke bread in the classroom together. During lunch, she did not address their disruptive behavior at all. She used the time to get to know them, to check in on how the students were doing, to ask what she could do to make the class more exciting, and to share information about herself that she had not shared with the rest of the class. After having lunch with these students, she learned that they liked her class but felt that she did not give them enough time to talk about what they were learning with their classmates. They also wanted to do more hands-on projects and more group work. Because Ms. Brewer invested time and a few dollars with her students outside of class time, she got to know them better and she learned from them how to improve the class from **their** perspective. The students got a chance to learn more about their teacher. This fundamentally changed their relationship and because she implemented much of what they suggested these students became more motivated to learn and more engaged in her class.

Finding time to eat lunch with students or even to sit next to them in the cafeteria during breakfast is one way for adults to break down the walls that serve as barriers to forging positive relationships with students. Many school leaders offer "Lunch with the Principal" as an incentive and while this is fine it often further marginalizes students because only the "good kids" have access to this opportunity. If we want to connect with all students, then we cannot use this only as a reward; it must be a strategy we leverage with all students, even the ones who drive us crazy because it is a great way to make personal connections with students.

Mr. Jackson

Mr. Jackson valued relationships with students because he remembered how important it was for him (as a student) to feel a sense of connection not just to his teachers but to the administrators and support staff at the schools he attended. He served as a math teacher at a large Midwest high school. Each year, he spent the first two weeks of class challenging students' self-perceptions that they were not "math people." He did this not by bombarding them with worksheets filled with formulas and word problems but by getting to know them as students. His mantra was "I cannot teach students that I do not know." So, despite conventional wisdom, he prioritized getting to know his students over content. He did this through formal mechanisms like student information and interest sheets but also by carving out time to check in with students before and after class. It was these short conversations about their day or the evening before where he forged bonds with his students. Not only did he learn something about them, but they learned about him as well. Their informal conversations led them to see that Mr. Jackson was not just a math teacher. He, like them, had nonacademic interests, had a sense of humor, and dealt with life's challenges. Each class period began with some sort of check-in. On some days it was simply asking, "Hey is everyone doing OK today?" and scanning the room to observe student verbal and nonverbal communication. On other days, he would facilitate a quick whip around, asking students to share how they were doing. He would allow students time to grapple with mathematical concepts individually and then in small groups and he would join groups to support students and encourage them to support one another. Because students felt safe in his class, and because he found ways to connect with them both during and outside of class, students worked for Mr. Jackson, and they allowed him to push them. One student, in particular, who benefitted from Mr. Jackson's emphasis on relationships, was Donovan. Donovan was an African American student who was recently diagnosed with ADHD. Donovan had issues with executive functioning and extreme disorganization. Rather than use Donovan's diagnosis and disorganization to accept his poor performance in his class, Mr. Jackson set daily after school meetings with him to discuss all of his classes. He required that Donvan use the school-provided agenda books to keep track of all his assignments; he provided Donovan with a binder to organize his course folders and made him complete a weekly log to ensure that Donovan submitted his assignments. Because of the trust that Mr. Jackson built with students like Donovan, they felt comfortable failing in front of him. They were willing to be vulnerable because of his intentionality in creating a learning community built on belonging and trust. Mr. Jackson's students consistently outperformed their peers because of the richness of the learning environment he created.

CHAPTER 4 SUMMARY

- The establishment of strong relationships with students must be a priority for all educators. This does not mean each adult in a school will know each student intimately, but it does mean that every child within a school should feel that there is at least one adult that they have a positive relationship with.

- Learning is an exercise in vulnerability. A prerequisite for vulnerability is the establishment of trust. Students do not

(Continued)

(Continued)

trust teachers they do not have a relationship with. What does this mean? Teachers who struggle to establish trusting relationships with students will also struggle to teach them.

- Most students, particularly marginalized students, and students who have a history of academic struggle are not motivated by grades. They value the relationships they have with their teachers and are motivated to work hard for teachers they have strong relationships with.

- Students want to have strong relationships with their teachers. Even the students who act like they do not. "The students who need love the most, often show it in the most unloving ways."

- School improvement efforts should begin not with an analysis of student performance data, but with an analysis of student–teacher relationships in the school.

REFLECTION QUESTIONS

1. What types of relationships did you have with your school administrators and teachers when you were a student? What is or are the name(s) of the adult(s) you had strong relationships with?

2. What strategies have you implemented to form relationships with students? What has worked well?

3. What barriers have you encountered when working to establish genuine relationships with students and their families? What have you done to overcome those barriers?

4. Do you feel comfortable establishing relationships with students who are different from you? Why or why not?

5. What actions can you and your school take tomorrow to ensure that every student feels that there is one adult that they have a genuine connection with?

The "E": Empowerment

LEARNING GOALS

As a result of reading this chapter, educators will:

☐ Realize that disempowering school cultures are manifestations of the thoughts, beliefs, and expectations of educators.

☐ Reflect on the unintentional and intentional ways schools disempower students.

☐ Be able to disrupt mindsets and end policies and practices that disempower students and families.

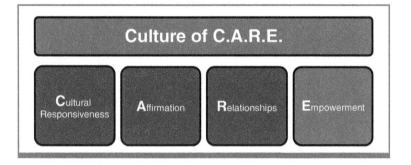

Out of the night that covers me,
Black as the pit from pole to pole,
I thank whatever gods may be
For my unconquerable soul.
In the fell clutch of circumstance
I have not winced nor cried aloud.
Under the bludgeonings of chance
My head is bloody, but unbowed.
Beyond this place of wrath and tears
Looms but the Horror of the shade,
And yet the menace of the years
Finds and shall find me unafraid.
It matters not how strait the gate,
How charged with punishments the scroll.
I am the master of my fate:
I am the captain of my soul.

—**William Ernest Henley (1875)**

Empowering Students to Take Control of Their Future

Invictus, written by William Ernest Henley, is recited daily by the students at Eagle Academy Bronx, a college preparatory public school that serves young men of color. Eagle Academy for Young Men was established in 2004 with a mission to "develop young men committed to the pursuit of academic excellence, strong character, and responsible leadership" (Rituals & Traditions, n.d.). What started as a single-site network in 2004, now operates four schools throughout New York City and Newark, New Jersey. The recitation of the poem *Invictus* reminds these young men of their power over their lives and that despite the toxic environmental conditions they may be subjected to, they have control of their futures. This ritual serves as an outright rejection of a victim's mentality, which consumes many young men living in poverty. It is one of many rituals that anchor the Eagle Academy for Young Men experience. The network founded by David Banks and now led by Donald Ruff (both African American men) has been unapologetic about the empowering nature of this network of schools, hiring men of color to lead the network's schools, ensuring representation in the teaching ranks, and even structuring the houses in the school to honor the legacies of powerful African American and Latino men. At the Bronx campus, for example, students are divided into houses: the Malcolm X House, the Che Guevara House, the Barack Obama House, and the Roberto Clemente House. These rituals and structures of empowerment are constant reminders that greatness, strength, and brilliance live within all of these young men (Banks, 2023). Girls on the Run, established in 1996 in Charlotte, North Carolina, is a nonprofit organization that partners with schools to empower girls in third through eighth grade. Its mission is to build the confidence and self-esteem of girls during one of the most vulnerable times in their lives. Through the promotion of physical activity (running) and social and emotional support, this program creates the conditions for girls to develop the armor necessary to thwart the constant bombardment and attacks on their self-image on social media and during school (Girls on the Run, 2023). Both Eagle Academy and Girls on the Run are working to empower two historically marginalized groups (young women and young men of color) through deliberate efforts to address their unique needs.

WHY EMPOWERMENT MATTERS

In the first four chapters of this book, I unpacked the first three pillars of the Culture of C.A.R.E. Framework: **C**ultural responsiveness, **A**ffirmation, and **R**elationships. I argued that a caring and nurturing school environment that promotes intellectual, social, emotional, and mental wellness must celebrate and respond to cultural diversity and affirm the identities of its students. I asserted that the relationship pillar ("R"), is the pillar upon which the others rest. Educators cannot be culturally responsive, or affirm students' identities without prioritizing and establishing positive relationships. This chapter focuses on the "E" of the Culture of C.A.R.E. Framework—"Empowerment." Empowering students is to help them realize their abilities and potential and grant them the power and authority to be great despite their circumstances. Empowering students requires that adults deeply interrogate their biases, prejudices and misconceptions about marginalized students and their families and that they surrender absolute control over the student experience to provide the opportunity and space for students to take greater ownership of their school-based experiences. Doing so builds student agency and efficacy. When students feel empowered in schools, they find meaning and relevance in the academic experience, leading to higher levels of engagement and productivity. When students are disempowered, they do not connect what they learn in school to their lived experiences, and they begin to see school as an institution of compliance rather than one of learning, development, and empowerment. In his best-selling book *Between the World and Me*, Ta-Nehisi Coates (2015) referred to the classroom as a "jail of other people's interests" (p. 48). For him and many students, particularly historically marginalized students, school becomes a place where academic success is contingent upon their willingness to abandon their interests and adopt an almost robotic disposition to survive school. How disempowering is that? Education in the United States is compulsory in most states until the age of sixteen or seventeen. Imagine having to spend six to seven hours each day in school, obligated to learn irrelevant skills, ideas, and concepts, and forced to learn in ways counter to how you learn best. When considering the empowerment pillar, educators must ask and answer this question honestly:

Is my desire for control and compliance creating disempowering learning experiences for students?

CONCRETE PRACTICES FOR OPERATIONALIZING EMPOWERMENT

For the remainder of this chapter, I will articulate how we unintentionally (and sometimes intentionally) disempower our students—and what we can do instead to empower students to own control of their futures. I will call out mindsets, policies, and practices that have maintained the status quo and drastically undermined students' academic experiences. With some interrogation and examination of the current state of schools, one will see that schools subscribe in practice to what Paulo Freire refers to as the banking concept of education (Freire, 2018). Students have become empty vessels by which educators deposit knowledge. Those who live on the margins in our schools are disempowered in both physical and intellectual ways. This disempowerment leads to disengagement and diminishes their natural inquisitiveness and curiosity.

Under the tremendously disempowering banking concept of education, Freire says:

a) the teacher teaches and the students are taught;
b) the teacher knows everything and the students know nothing;
c) the teacher thinks and the students are thought about;
d) the teacher talks and the students listen – meekly;
e) the teacher disciplines and the students are disciplined;
f) the teacher chooses and enforces the choice, and the students comply;
g) the teacher acts and the students have the illusion of acting, through the action of the teacher;
h) the teacher chooses the program content, and the students (who were not consulted) adapt to it;

i) the teacher confuses the authority of knowledge with his or her own professional authority, which he or she sets in opposition to the freedom of the students;

j) the teacher is the subject of the learning process, while the pupils are mere objects. (Freire, 2018, p. 73)

Even though these words were penned in the late 1960s, they remain a strikingly accurate description of today's educative process, particularly in schools that serve marginalized children. This, coupled with a host of other problematic practices and deficit thinking, has made for a disempowering experience for many students. As I call out these problematic mindsets and practices, I will offer ways of thinking and strategies to empower students in ways that will recharge their thirst for knowledge, understanding, and increase their sense of belonging.

Empowering Practice #1: Empower Adults

Disempowered adults, disempowered children. Empowering students requires that school leaders first empower the adults that serve them. Principals, if you lead a school with a lack of collective ownership and shared accountability, then you are leading a culture of disempowerment. Students will not thrive in environmental conditions like this. Regardless of their title and job description, adults in a school want to feel that their perspectives are honored and that the expertise and experiential knowledge they possess is honored. Far too often, teachers feel like subjects within a kingdom rather than leaders of an organization. Feelings of powerlessness, disillusionment, and frustration impact the quality of their work experience which has a negative effect on the children they serve. Curricular decisions should rarely, if ever, be made without the input of the teachers who will be most impacted by it. Operational and logistical decisions should rarely be made without consulting those responsible for executing the plans. School leaders who empower the adults they lead and serve are adept at hiring the right people, resist micromanagement, and build teams as extensions of themselves to provide the necessary leadership and support to operate the school effectively (Khalifa, 2018). Teacher and staff have voice and can offer suggestions and ideas that improve both the experiences and the performance of the students they serve. Empowering principals view leadership as an organizational property, not something contained within one individual entity.

Empowering Practice #2: Empower Families and Broaden the Definition of Family Engagement

Students know what you think about their families, not by what you say but by how you treat them. They know which families have the social and political capital and those who do not. Schools in marginalized communities often see families as part of the problem, not part of the solution. I certainly felt that way as a young turnaround principal in Chicago. When I assumed control of the Sherman School of Excellence in the Fall of 2006, I was openly critical of the parent community and I even publicly made statements such as, "If parents did what they were supposed to do, I wouldn't be here." There were some issues that I had to address as it relates to how parents engaged with teachers and school personnel. There were certainly some parents who behaved in a manner that was antithetical to the type of school culture we were trying to create, but my approach to addressing these parents could have been different. My approach was rooted in deficit thinking. Rather than limit family access to the school, I needed to figure out ways to support parents in engaging with the school and teachers in productive and positive ways. This takes time that principals do not have, but as I always remind aspiring leaders, you will put the time in on the front end or the back end; it is your choice. When parents and families are mistreated, devalued, and unwelcome by schools, their children see and feel it, and this mistreatment impacts them in myriad ways. It shows up in their lack of commitment to school and lack of trust in the school leaders and teachers, making it difficult to partner with families to provide much-needed student support. School leaders and teachers must find ways to engage families authentically. Too often schools only engage parents when students are misbehaving or when they need them to show up to Individualized Educational Plan (IEP) meetings.

We must broaden the definition of *family engagement*. Attendance at open house, report card pick-up, and parent–teacher conferences are insufficient mechanisms to gauge family engagement levels or a family's commitment to their child's education. Far too often, schools label families as not caring about or not valuing education because of the inability of the family to be present at these events. Not only do schools have to broaden their definitions of family involvement and engagement there needs to be a shared understanding of what schools want families to be involved or engaged in.

> Family engagement for what?

Educators must grapple with this question: What do we want parents and families to do to support their students? Once there is clarity around the purpose of parent and family engagement, then school leaders, in concert with teachers and staff, can provide opportunities for family engagement. In Grand Rapids, Michigan, schools enlisted the assistance of grandmas and grandpas to help end bullying. These senior citizen volunteers were trained to identify and prevent bullying from persisting in schools (Scott, 2012). A high school in Shreveport, Louisiana, started the *Dads on Duty* program and enlisting fathers to leverage positive male presence to reduce fighting and behavioral infractions in schools. Some dads offer an encouraging smile; others provide direct mentoring and tutoring services (Fanning, 2023). I have worked with leaders of elementary schools in Chicago that use parents to improve academic outcomes through parent mentoring programs. Schools are training moms, dads, and other custodial family members to facilitate small-group instruction and one-to-one tutoring to help improve student achievement. Other schools are using their Parent Advisory Councils and "Friends of…" groups to address attendance issues, fundraise for special programming, and hire additional teachers. In each example, the school had a specific purpose behind family involvement and created a specific program to be able to do that. These involved families are the best sources of knowledge of their children and their community. When students see their families actively involved in their education, they feel more empowered, have an increased desire to achieve, and are less likely to engage in destructive behaviors. It also sends a message that their family and community do not need to be fixed and that just like their school leaders and principals they can also contribute to the school community in meaningful ways.

Empowering Practice #3: Disrupt Racialized Hierarchies

In Chapter 3, I mention the importance of empowering teachers and staff of color. This is important because the disruption of the racialized hierarchies is essential to the empowerment of marginalized students. Schools are a microcosm of society, and as marginalized children navigate U.S. society, they notice who is in charge. They recognize it is often not the people who look like them. They notice that many restaurants and stores they patronize are not owned by people who look like them. The doctors and nurses who tend to them do not look like them. The police officers they interact with on the street do not look like them. This reality, like the racialized hierarchal structure of schools, disempowers them. Eighty percent of school principals are white, and of that number, 80% are male. Teacher demographics are similar, with 80% identifying as white and female (National Center for Education Statistics, 2023). Students not only notice the lack of representation in the teaching and school leadership ranks, but they also notice who in their schools has the power, and they know that it is often not the adults who look like them. Even in schools, for example, that serve mostly students of color and the school principal is a person of color, the often predominantly white teaching staff wields a tremendous amount of power and authority over the students' experiences. As I mentioned in Chapter 3, educators must be mindful of the subliminal messages sent to historically marginalized children. Students only believe they can be what they see. If they only see representatives of themselves in schools sweeping floors, serving mashed potatoes, or policing them, they begin to form disempowering self-perceptions that limit what they believe they can be. Disruption of the racialized hierarchy requires that school leaders be intentional about hiring and retaining teachers of color by taking control over the hiring process. Many school leaders surrender control of hiring processes to their teachers. While this is a great way of distributing leadership to teacher teams and empowering teachers to make decisions, it often becomes a barrier to diversifying the staff. Teacher teams often hire those whom they feel a personal connection with, not necessarily who is the best candidate for the children they serve. White teachers are more likely to recommend the hiring of other white teachers. School leaders must be willing to assess the composition of their staff and ensure that there is greater representation within the school and be willing to make adults uncomfortable to do what is right by children. While the pool of qualified teacher candidates of color is small, schools and districts must "grow their own" (see Chapter 2) and be willing to form partnerships with local colleges and universities and Historically Black Colleges and Universities, support programs like Call Me Mister, and encourage their students of color to enter the teaching profession (like Dr. Bloland did me).

To address the dearth of leaders of color in education, schools, and districts must be committed to providing authentic leadership opportunities for however many teachers and staff members of color they have. The return on this investment will result in an increased number of candidates of color in the leadership talent pool. In 2020, I cofounded and helped design the Aspire Fellowship to address the lack of diversity in the principal pipeline. Born out of a partnership between the University of Illinois at Chicago's Urban Education Leadership and Teach for America (2023), the fellowship is a ten-month program that supports the development of teacher leaders of color and prepares them to gain admission into principal certification programs. Disruption of racialized hierarchies in schools to empower historically marginalized students in ways that free them to reach their full potential.

Empowering Practice #4: Acknowledge the Power of Socialization and Its Implications

As school leaders, teachers, and support staff, we must acknowledge how we have all been socialized into believing in the inherent inferiority of historically marginalized people, particularly African Americans and Latinx. Irby (2021) argues that many teachers are socialized "to not believe and believe in Black and Brown students" and that many educators believe African Americans and Latinx are "perpetually dishonest or at best lack the capacity to be right" (p. 27). My work with school leaders across the country has revealed that in schools that serve African American, Latinx, and children who are economically disadvantaged, there is often a hyperfocus on compliance and control. The children in these schools are often victims of assumed deviancy and targeted exclusion (Anderson, 2019). We find this especially true of African American boys who are labeled as problem children as early as pre-kindergarten. When a child is labeled deviant, an educator is going to be much more concerned with monitoring their behavior and controlling their bodies, often at the expense of educating their minds.

Socialization is powerful and leaders and teachers must accept that this socialization bleeds into their minds and hearts and influences their interactions with the students and families they serve. Even good-hearted, well-intentioned educators of color fall victim to the power of socialization. In his book *Culturally Responsive School Leadership*, Muhammad Khalifa (2018), an African American male professor and scholar, recounts that as a middle school science teacher, he too, fell victim to this socialization:

> Unfortunately, early on, I was socialized into accepting deficit-based understandings about many of these poor and minoritized students … Therefore, through my own ignorance, it was easy for me to accept the deficit narratives that my more experienced mentor colleagues passed my way … So there I was, myself an educated Black man from a socially conscious Black 'protest' family, deciding to teach in Detroit to help impoverished Black students, and I was guilty as charged: I held and espoused deficit-oriented constructions of Black (and other minoritized) students and I pathologized segments of our communities. (pp. 1–2)

The socialization that Khalifa speaks of, and the fear often associated with communities of color lead to the implementation of policies and the employment of practices that blur the line between schools and prisons. This school-to-prison nexus suggests that "instead of simply steering students toward incarceration, there are myriad practices that schools and prisons have in common, which condition us to see people of color as inherently dangerous and in need of constant monitoring" (Stumbo, 2019). I am aware of how socialization and pathologic narratives can influence educator's thinking about the students and families they serve because I was one of those educators.

As a turnaround principal in Chicago, I assumed control of the second worst-performing school in the state of Illinois. No Child Left Behind Legislation granted authority to the state of Illinois and Chicago Public Schools, which were under mayoral control, to close and turn around schools that were deemed low performing. The school, which was located on the south side of Chicago, suffered from a culture of dysfunction, demoralization, and disinvestment. I assumed the school's leadership and transformed into Joe Clark 2.0. A big fan of the 1989 movie starring Morgan Freeman as Joe Clark, the principal of Eastside High School in Paterson, New Jersey, I was ready to transform the school. During the movie, "Crazy Joe" Clark utilizes controversial measures to wrestle back control of the school from gangsters, drug dealers, and wayward students who were blamed for the dysfunctional school environment. In my eyes, Joe Clark was a hero. So, while I did not force students to sing the school song on demand or walk around with a Louisville Slugger, I employed practices that resembled those you would find in prisons. We had metal detectors and wands to screen students as they entered the building in the morning. Students were forced to wear uniforms. I would initiate random searches of students' bookbags. We implemented a silent hallway policy (regardless of age or grade level, students could not chat in the hallways). Student movement was highly restricted. For example, students had to walk up the right side of the staircase and down the left side. In the hallways, in addition to being silent, students had to walk one to a square, and when standing in line, some teachers had them walk with their hands behind their backs or holding a book. Sadly, I even used carceral terms like *lockdown* and *sweeps* when I wanted the security team to clear hallways of students and limit student movement around the building. If you have ever seen the inside of a prison, inmates are moved from one area to another similarly. When groups of students or classes were engaged in disruptive behaviors, we would punish them by taking away their recess time, much like prisoners who misbehave have their "yard" time taken away. Unfortunately, it was not just my school. Other schools in Chicago fined students when their shirts were not tucked in or if they were missing a belt or the proper shoes. These fines would compound yearly and jeopardize a student's ability to matriculate to the next grade or even graduate. Thankfully, we are starting to see schools and school districts move away from zero-tolerance policies, but the mindset still exists. Some leaders and teachers want a pound of flesh for any transgression a student makes or any sign of disrespect or noncompliance. Unfortunately, some schools even want to legislate how students sit at their desks. Behavior management systems like SLANT, which on the surface appear reasonable, end up becoming another example of an oppressive ritual that exists in schools that further strengthens the grasp that schools have over the bodies of marginalized students. SLANT requires that students Sit up, Listen, Ask questions, Nod, and Track the Speaker. Sounds good, right? Not if it simply becomes another compliance mechanism. One also must consider that the implication of the implementation of SLANT is that marginalized students do not know how to sit at a desk during class. Even as schools and districts move away from overly punitive disciplinary policies and relax dress codes and appearance requirements, there is still an overemphasis on control and compliance under the guise of safety and inclusivity. Discipline and achievement data reveal that school remains a hostile place for historically marginalized students (Khalifa, 2018). African American, Latinx, mixed-race students, or students who live in poverty are much more likely to be overly punished for behaviors that are deemed disrespectful or disruptive or be victimized by the inequitable enforcement of school policies. The elimination of policies alone will not lead to school cultures that are less control centered and compliance heavy because, as I have articulated, policies do not legislate what is in the hearts of educators. Those who fear marginalized students or those who subscribe to bias and stereotypes find comfort in policies and practices that legislate how certain students walk, talk, and dress. Effectively addressing the root cause of our infatuation and dependency on using punitive methodologies to compel students to act in ways that make adults more comfortable requires educators to critically examine their beliefs, thoughts, and understandings about historically marginalized students.

Uniform and dress code policies are another disempowering mechanism that schools employ. It is also a clear example of the inequities that are baked into the public school system. In the 1980s and 1990s, when nonprivate schools began to require that students wear uniforms, two justifications were given: (1) student safety (2) and eliminating distractions through the removal of peer pressure and intrastudent class-ism. Street organizations were highly organized in the 1980s and 1990s and had formal structures. Students often expressed their allegiances through the colors that they wore. The argu-ment that forcing students to wear uniforms keeps them safe is now outdated, as the collapse of these highly structured and organized gangs means they are no longer identifiable by colors as they once were. Uniforms have never protected children and have never prevented a student from being fought, jumped, or shot. The argument that uniforms relieve students of peer pressure as it blurs the line between the haves and have-nots is overstated. Even with uniforms, it is easy to distinguish between students living in or below poverty and those who are not. One can see the student who wears the same uniform shirt and pants daily versus those who cycle through multiple pairs of shirts and pants and can accessorize with fancy belts and the latest Jordans. So, if uniforms do not keep children safe, and they do not prevent peer pressure or low self-esteem due to poverty, then why do many schools that serve marginalized children require them? Control. Not only do educators want to legislate how a student sits in class, but they also want to legislate the clothes they wear and how they wear their hair. This obsession with control and compli-ance creates disempowering and, in some cases, traumatic experiences for historically marginalized students. There have been cases across the country where young women have been targeted by dress codes that many deem sexist and unfair (Clayburn, 2022). A young African American male student in

Mont Belvieu, Texas, was suspended not once but twice from school for wearing locs despite state legislation outlawing racial discrimination based on hairstyles (Mayorquin, 2023), and in Kansas, an eight-year-old Native American boy, whose family is a member of the Wyandotte Nation was forced to cut his hair to comply his school's hair policy (Somasundaram, 2023). These are just a few examples of how these policies harm marginalized students. Educators must ask if the enforcement of these policies, which are often rooted in racism and classism are worth the pain that students are put through. Do they result in the intended outcome? And finally, would these types of policies ever be enforced in predominantly white schools? It is important for school leaders and teachers to question why, for example, students are not allowed to wear hoodies. Is banning the hoodie or any article of clothing or style about protecting the learning environment, or is it about something deeper and perhaps more sinister? Are students who wear hoodies less likely to learn or negatively impact the learning of others? Every time we enact a policy or practice that dictates what a student can wear, their hairstyle, how they sit at a desk, and how they walk through a hallway, we are attacking their self-expression and diminishing their sense of self. That is disempowering.

Empowering Practice #5: Reject Deficit Language

You will notice that I use the phrase *historically marginalized* to identify the groups of students who would benefit most from the establishment of a Culture of C.AR.E. I use this term rather than at-risk, challenged, or troubled because it most accurately describes these students as part of a community that has been forced to live and exist on the margins of society. These same students also live on the margins in our schools and are denied access to the full depth and breadth of the school experience. They lack full-curricular or extra-curricular access, and they are less likely to enroll in AP or Honors courses, join the school band, the debate team or serve on the student council.

How we speak and think about children influences how we interact with them, the urgency we have for their development, our commitment to their success, and the quality of the instruction we provide. Teacher perceptions matter as they shape the academic experiences and how students see themselves in school. Low expectations disempower students. A 2015 report on the power of teacher perceptions and expectations revealed that race and class deeply influence teachers' perceptions of their students' abilities. The study revealed that non-African American teachers of Black students have significantly lower expectations than African American teachers (Rubie-Davies et al., 2015).

It is time to bury terms like *achievement gap* and *attitude gap*. These are just two terms that are part of a language of education that absolves educators of any responsibility for students' academic struggles and disparate achievement rates. Even though the educational community has largely moved away from deficit-laden terms, the thinking that accompanies these terms persists. People are becoming more careful about what they say but have not necessarily changed their thoughts. The achievement gap, as I argued in my 2019 speech titled "The Achievement Gap Is Fake News" (Allen and Illinois Principal Association, 2019) at the Illinois Principal Association Fall Conference, is problematic. Firstly, it forces marginalized students and families to center the performance of white students as the goal for achievement. This breeds a feeling of inferiority and the idea "that something must be wrong with us." It further pathologizes marginalized students and socializes educators, even the well-intentioned ones, to believe that there is something inherently wrong with them and that these students need to be fixed. Secondly, using the term *achievement gap* frames the problem as merely a performance issue. This oversimplification does not illuminate the root causes of performance disparities in schools and school districts.

The term *attitude gap* is problematic because a major part of Kafele's (2013) theory places the blame for student failure on the students. It implies that if marginalized students had better attitudes and more will to succeed, they would perform better in school. I agree that teachers need to explore their attitudes about marginalized students, but I do not agree that student attitudes should be a part of that discussion. Students often have legitimate reasons to have bad attitudes. This idea and those who champion it fail to critically examine the systems and structures that perpetuate inequities in schools and the attitudes, beliefs, and mindsets that serve as roadblocks to the type of deep-seated change that is necessary in schools. These same thoughts are why I was an opponent of the movement to teach children grit. Let's play this thinking out. Resourceful and resilient children who battle through significant challenges just to come to school every day need to be taught grit and persistence by educators, many of whom grew up middle class? Yeah, OK. The thinking is similar: If students had more grit and persistence and just tried harder, they would be more successful in school. It is so much easier to point the finger at students rather than own that the culture that has been created in schools that lead to unintended outcomes, disproportionality, and disempowerment.

Empowering Practice #6: Prioritize Choice, Growth, and Learning Over Grading

Yes, I am saying the quiet part out loud: Grades do not really matter, and they do more harm than good. The collective emphasis on grading and using those grades to compare and categorize students is disempowering. I have worked at and with many schools over my almost twenty-five years in education, and I cannot think of a year when grading or grading philosophies were not a topic of conversation. If I were appointed the king of all things in education, one of my first decisions would be eliminating grades. They evoke confusion, stress, and anxiety and often fail to capture a student's ability or academic potential. A young man I played high school basketball against a young man that had a 4.5 GPA and made the Honor Roll every semester. When he sat for the ACT, he scored a 14. Even with test anxiety, with a 4.5 GPA, he should have been able to score higher than a 14 on the ACT. Grades often paint false or inaccurate pictures of what students are capable of and can erroneously inflate a student's academic self-esteem or destroy it. In far too many schools, teachers weaponize their grade books and use them to ensure compliance. Compliant students earn good grades, noncompliant students receive bad grades, regardless of their ability to demonstrate proficiency or mastery.

Grading fosters an environment of competition and comparison, which would be fine if schools were a meritocracy, and the playing fields were level. Because that is not the case, it is tremendously disempowering to place so much emphasis on grades as a tool to compare students. With this overemphasis on competition and comparison, schools, which should be disrupting the status quo and serving as the great equalizer, simply reproduce social inequities and sort students into categories based on their grades, the tracks they are placed in, and their standardized test scores.

Recognizing that society is not prepared to do away with grades, I suggest that school leaders and teachers work collaboratively to build a culture of learning and growth. In this type of culture, students explore how they learn best and how they demonstrate what they learn best. Despite technological advancements, schools have simply swapped paper and pencils for laptops and touchpads. Giving students a choice in how they would like to learn a particular topic or how they would like to master a standard or set of objectives would be tremendously empowering. Giving them a choice in how they demonstrate mastery or proficiency is also empowering. When teaching history in the early aught years, I provided multiple ways for students to show me what they learned. For an end-of-unit assessment on the colonial period, students could respond to a set of essay questions or create an annotated timeline, a cartoon, or produce a news segment. For the Civil War unit, I had students adopt a profile of someone who lived during that time and create a scrapbook from that person's perspective. We debated in class whether the United States should have dropped the atomic bomb on Hiroshima and Nagasaki, and we used primary resources to construct artifacts when learning about the civil rights movement and Vietnam. Students feel empowered when they are granted agency and self-direction in their educational journey.

We must also acknowledge growth and effort. Schools that empower students understand that many of the benchmarks we use to track and stratify students are arbitrary and do not account for the reality that students grow and develop intellectually at different rates. When we acknowledge growth, celebrations of achievement become more inclusive. When we celebrate effort, they become even more inclusive. When students are rewarded for their effort, they put in more effort, which will improve outcomes (Perry et al., 2003). Schools that seek to empower students will find ways to not just reward static performance but also celebrate students who are making progress and putting in effort even if they still are coming up short on hitting the target.

CHAPTER 5 SUMMARY

- Empowering students means helping them realize their abilities and potential and granting them the power and authority to be great despite their circumstances.

- School leaders who want to develop empowering schools for students must also empower the adults who serve them.

- Educators who feel sorry for their students, have low expectations, or despise them and their families will fail to empower their students.

- Empowering educators deeply reflect on their biases, prejudices, and misconceptions about marginalized students and their families and consider how their beliefs shape their students' experiences.

- Educators must be willing to surrender absolute control over the student experience and provide the opportunity and space for students to take greater ownership of their school-based experiences.

REFLECTION QUESTIONS

1. Reflect on your experiences as a student. How were you empowered or disempowered in school?

2. What predispositions, biases, and prejudices do you harbor toward historically marginalized students and their families?

3. How might your school be unintentionally disempowering students? Think about school rules, policies, staffing, and so on.

4. What are the barriers to student empowerment?

5. What can you begin to do tomorrow as a teacher or school leader to empower students?

CHAPTER SIX

Conclusion

They didn't drop out, they were pushed out.

Pushed Out

Let me tell the story of Ahmad and Angel, an African American boy and a Latino boy who had problems sitting on the reading rug and focusing during story time in their pre-kindergarten classrooms. Their teacher, who struggled to channel their rambunctious but innocent energy, complained incessantly about their behaviors. As the complaints persisted, the principal approved a set of exclusionary tactics that would be used to appease the teacher and limit the

(Continued)

93

(Continued)

distractions that Ahmad and Angel were causing. It began with having them picked up early from school; the suspensions started when that did not work. When the behaviors did not improve to the teacher's liking, the days of suspension increased. Ahmad and Angel missed over a third of the school year due to "early dismissals" and suspensions. These boys were labeled troubled children. No one called them that, but they treated them as such. The labels followed them to kindergarten and first grade, where the patterns of early dismissals and suspensions continued. Ahmad and Angel's families grew increasingly frustrated by their children's hypervisibility. It appeared that Ahmad and Angel could not breathe without punishment. As the frustration mounted, they began to step back. They began to lose trust that the school had their sons' best interests in mind. Years after, through the intermediate grades and middle school, these boys, now growing into young men, had to deal with the ramifications of the perceptions teachers had of them, and as those perceptions shaped them and their academic experiences, they began to exhibit the behaviors that teachers expected of them. By high school, Ahmad and Angel had become what teachers said they were in pre-K. Rather than be treated as criminals, they rarely attended school, they figured that this was what the adults wanted anyway. The adultification of their behaviors before they could even read, feeling targeted by the adults who were supposed to care for them, and never receiving the benefit of the doubt or being offered a second chance, had finally become too much. By junior year, Ahmad and Angel, who were once excited little boys who struggled to sit on the reading rug, were now young men in rival gangs running the streets, living day to day and struggling to survive. Their school administrators coded them as dropouts in the attendance system, but these young men did not drop out; Ahmad and Angel were pushed out.

If we do not address the toxicity of the soil that our students are planted in, they will never grow to achieve their full potential.

A CULTURE OF C.A.R.E. MATTERS

Stories like this are all too familiar in our schools and districts. Ahmad and Angel are two of many. Swap out the names, and this is the story of African American, Latinx, rural white children, homeless, and many other types of children who find themselves not wanted in their schools because they are from economically depressed communities, speak English as a second language or have parents who work multiple jobs and cannot be a constant presence in the school. Ahmads and Angels are not born; they are made. A way to avoid the persistence of stories like this is to ensure that schools establish cultures built on cultural responsiveness, affirmation, relationships, and empowerment (C.A.R.E.).

In this book, I argued that if schools establish a Culture of C.A.R.E., they will dramatically improve the academic experience of often marginalized student groups, leading to improved outcomes. All students benefit from establishing a Culture of C.A.R.E., but historically marginalized students benefit more because their school experiences are often undermined by invisibility or assumed deviancy. Expecting students to thrive in these environments is irrational, yet much of our school improvement work addresses student outcomes. Achievement disparities and unintended outcomes result from deeper systemic and cultural issues that must be addressed. If we do not address the toxicity of the soil that our students are planted in, they will never grow to achieve their full potential. We have adopted a "kid-fixing" mentality in education, where the strategies are all geared to what children (and families) need to do differently to improve outcomes. We blame families and students when attendance rates are low, and class cut rates are high. We say students do not come to school because their families do not value education. We are argue that students cut class because they do not care about their grades or care about their futures. We rarely ask ourselves if students elect not to attend school because they feel mistreated, isolated, or uncared for. We rarely ask ourselves why a student never misses Mrs. Jones's class but constantly cuts Mr. Williams's class.

GROWTH EMERGES FROM DISCOMFORT

I hope this book made you a bit uncomfortable. Growth will only emerge from discomfort. As educational leaders, teachers, and staff members, we owe it to ourselves to ask tough questions that force us to carefully examine our mindsets, practices, and how we engage with our students and families. For too long, we have prioritized the comfort and convenience of adults over what we know is best for students. We already know what we must do; the question is, do we, as an educational community, have the courage to do it? Suppose school leaders, teachers, and staff are committed to disrupting the systems that produce adverse outcomes for certain groups of students. In that case, we must be willing to reject traditional ways of thinking about and doing the business of schooling. Let us surrender our focus on measurable outcomes and examine the health of our school culture and the systems that consistently produce the outcomes that we say are unintended.

EDUCATORS CONTROL SCHOOL CULTURE

Nick Saban, one of the winningest coaches in college football history, once said that in sports and life, we focus too much on outcomes and not enough on the process. According to Saban, no banners or posters in the University of Alabama Football complex say "Win the championship" or "Be undefeated," even though Alabama has gone undefeated twice and won the national championship six times under his leadership. Instead, he says, you will see reminders about paying attention to detail, practicing purposefully, working hard, and taking advantage of each day to improve (Arkansas Business, 2021). The University of Alabama's football team has a winning culture. Coach Saban admits he does not control the game's outcome, even as a winning coach. He controls how well his team is prepared, the coaches' and players' attentiveness to their roles and responsibilities, and the program's culture. If he does all this right, the outcomes will care for themselves. This same line of thinking should be applied to education. There are so many things that educators have no control over. We do not control whether a family reads to their children at night or provides a quiet place for the child to study or do homework; we do not control whether a child has been exposed to trauma; we do not control poverty or unemployment rates, yet educators have a tremendous amount of control over the *culture of the school* and the experiences that children have in schools. What if, along with the posters with attendance and academic performance goals, we also had posters to remind adults to be nice to children, to make their lessons fun, to make every child feel good, and to value relationships? What happens within the four walls of a school is under the control of the adults who work there. School culture is within their control, the quality of instruction is within their control, and the mindsets toward students and their families are in their control. Establishing a Culture of C.A.R.E. requires first that you acknowledge your power and be willing to channel that power and the authority you have been granted to improve the school experiences of the children you serve.

Consider establishing a culture of C.A.R.E. in your school because it will benefit all students, and all it takes from you is desire, will, and commitment. Resist the infatuation with strategies, if we want to improve our schools it begins with establishing the right culture. As Peter Drucker once said, culture eats strategy for breakfast.

References

Allen, A., Scott, L. M., & Lewis, C. W. (2013). Racial microaggressions and African American and Hispanic students in urban schools: A call for culturally affirming education. *The Journal of Teaching and Learning, 3*(2), 117–129.

Allen, L., & Illinois Principal Association. (2019, November 9). *The achievement gap and other fake news: IGNITE Talks.* https://www.youtube.com/watch?v=oQaCum9hdrI

Anderson, R. (2019). *Wassup with all the Black boys sitting in the principal's office.* Black Boy Wonder.

Arkansas Business. (2021, April 27). *Nick Saban's tips for success, in football and business* [Video]. Arkansas Business. https://www.arkansasbusiness.com/article/video-nick-sabans-tips-for-success-in-football-and-business/#:~:text=%E2%80%9CPeople%20want%20to%20focus%20on

Baldwin, J. (1963, October 16). *The Negro child: His self-Image.* https://richgibson.com/talktoteachers.htm

Banas, C., & Byers, D. (1987, November 7). Chicago's schools hit as worst. *Chicago Tribune.* https://www.chicagotribune.com/news/ct-xpm-1987-11-07-8703230806-story.html

Banks, D. C. (2023). *Rituals & traditions.* https://www.eaglebronx.org/for-scholars-families/rituals-traditions

Bonilla-Silva, E. (2010). *Racism without racists: Color-blind racism and the persistence of racial inequality in the United States.* Rowman & Littlefield.

Buchanan-Rivera, E. (2022). *Identity affirming classrooms.* Routledge.

Cascio, C. N., O'Donnell, M. B., Tinney, F. J., Lieberman, M. D., Taylor, S. E., Strecher, V. J., & Falk, E. B. (2015). Self-affirmation activates brain systems associated with self-related processing and reward and is reinforced by future orientation. *Social Cognitive and Affective Neuroscience, 11*(4), 621–629. https://doi.org/10.1093/scan/nsv136

Chicago Public Schools. (2005). *School quality rating policy results and accountability status 2005.* https://www.cps.edu/about/district-data/metrics/accountability-reports/

Clayburn, C. (2022, December 23). *Why school dress codes are often unfair.* U.S. News & World Report. https://www.usnews.com/education/best-high-schools/articles/why-school-dress-codes-are-often-unfair

Clear, J. (2018). *Atomic habits.* Penguin.

Coates, T.-N. (2015). *Between the world and me*. Random House.

Comer, J. (2001). Schools that develop children. *The American Prospect, 12*(7), 33–35.

Douglass Horsford, S. (2011). *Learning in a burning house: Educational inequality, ideology, and (dis)integration*. Teachers College Press.

Edmonds, R. (1979). Effective schools for the urban poor. *Educational Leadership, 37*, 15–24.

Ewing, E. L. (2018). *Ghosts in the schoolyard: Racism and school closings on Chicago's South side*. The University of Chicago Press.

Fanning, C. (2023, July 14). *These fathers formed "Dads on Duty" to prevent violence at a local high school*. Reader's Digest. https://www.rd.com/list/dads-on-duty/

Freire, P. (2018). *Pedagogy of the oppressed*. 50th Anniv. ed. Bloomsbury Academic. (Original work published 1970)

Gershenson, S., Hart, C., Lindsay, C., & Papageorge, N. W. (2017). The long-run impacts of same-race teachers. *SSRN Electronic Journal*. https://doi.org/10.2139/ssrn.2940620

Girls on the Run. (2023). *What we do: After school running program for girls*. GOTR. https://www.girlsontherun.org/what-we-do/

Henley, W. E. (1875). *Invictus*. https://www.poetry.com/poem/40493/invictus

Irby, D. J. (2021). *Stuck improving: Racial equity and school leadership*. Harvard Education Press.

Kafele, B. K. (2013). *Closing the attitude gap: How to fire up your students to strive for success*. ASCD.

Khalifa, M. A. (2018). *Culturally responsive school leadership*. Harvard Education Press.

Labaree, D. F. (2010). *Someone has to fail: The zero-sum game of public schooling*. Harvard University Press. https://doi.org/10.2307/j.ctvjk2wpb

Ladson-Billings, G. (1994). *The dreamkeepers: Successful teachers of African American children*. Jossey-Bass.

Mayorquin, O. (2023, December 6). Black student in Texas is suspended over hair length again. *The New York Times*. https://www.nytimes.com/2023/12/05/us/darryl-george-hair-locs-texas.html

Milner, R. (2006). The promise of Black teachers' success with Black students. *Educational Foundations, 20*(3), 89–104.

Muhammad, G. (2020). *Cultivating genius: An equity framework for culturally and historically responsive literacy*. Scholastic.

National Center for Education Statistics. (2023). *Characteristics of public and private school principals. Condition of Education*. U.S. Department of Education, Institute of Education Sciences. https://nces.ed.gov/programs/coe/indicator/cls

Nin, A., & Jarczok, A. (2014). Seduction of the minotaur. Swallow Press/Ohio University Press.

Novak, S. (2023, January 12). Half of the 250 kids expelled from preschool each day are Black boys. *Scientific American.* https://www.scientificamerican.com/article/half-of-the-250-kids-expelled-from-preschool-each-day-are-black-boys/

Perry, T., Steele, C., & Hilliard, A. G. (2003). *Young, gifted, and black: Promoting high achievement among African-American students.* Beacon.

Pierson, R. (2013, May). *Every kid needs a champion* [Video]. TED Talks. https://www.ted.com/talks/rita_pierson_every_kid_needs_a_champion

Rose, J. (2012, May 9). How to break free of our 19th-century factory-model education system. *The Atlantic.* https://www.theatlantic.com/business/archive/2012/05/how-to-break-free-of-our-19th-century-factory-model-education-system/256881/

Rubie-Davies, C. M., Peterson, E. R., Sibley, C. G., & Rosenthal, R. (2015). A teacher expectation intervention: Modelling the practices of high expectation teachers. *Contemporary Educational Psychology, 40,* 72–85. https://doi.org/10.1016/j.cedpsych.2014.03.003

Scott, M. (2012). *Watch out school bullies: Grandma and grandpa are on patrol.* Mlive. https://www.mlive.com/news/grand-rapids/2012/04/watch_out_school_bullies_grand.html

Somasundaram, P. (2023, November 26). Kansas school forced Native American student to cut his hair, ACLU says. *Washington Post.* https://www.washingtonpost.com/nation/2023/11/21/native-american-student-hair-aclu/

Stumbo, C. (2019). Understanding the school-to-prison nexus (Blog). https://westwinded.com/blog/understanding-the-school-to-prison-nexus/

Teach for America. (2023). *Aspire fellowship.* https://www.tfachicagonwi.org/aspire-fellowship

Willcox, G. (1982). The feeling wheel, *Transactional Analysis Journal, 12*(4), 274–276. https://doi.org/10.1177/036215378201200411

Wilkerson, I. (2020). *Caste.* Allen Lane.

Williford, A. P., Álamos, P., Whittaker, J., & Accavitti, M. R. (2023). Missing out: Kindergarten teachers' reports of soft exclusionary discipline practices. *Early Education and Development,* 1–20. https://doi.org/10.1080/10409289.2023.2291745

Index

A Sage Company

CORWIN HAS ONE MISSION: to enhance education through intentional professional learning.

We build long-term relationships with our authors, educators, clients, and associations who partner with us to develop and continuously improve the best evidence-based practices that establish and support lifelong learning.